"These 'Sips' of wisdom from the WineSpirit community nourish us as they quietly guide us to a richer sense of self. Wine is an apt metaphor in the search for deeper meaning and fulfillment. The grape is crushed, fermented, and reborn as a lovely beverage able to develop and mature at a pace undreamt of by other agricultural products. So, too, we humans are shaped, broken and remolded by life and its endless circumstances. By example, wine brings us closer to the mystery of who we are.

"More often than not, the shared world we live in survives on 'fast food' forms of wisdom that distract from our true selves. In many ways our spirit's quest is to more fully understand who we are and our relationship to life. Reading these short communiqués from the vineyard front reminds us that taking the time to ask real questions supports our desire to know ourselves with greater clarity and compassion."

-Burke Owens, Director of Communications, Bonny Doon Vineyard, Sommelier

"Within Biblical tradition, wine, like bread, is a quintessential food: a food for the body, a food for the soul. Our ancestors made it part of their most sacred moments, times set apart from the day-to-day world. A good wine, a good friend, a quiet moment: together, these essential components of our lives give life meaning. Americans tend to look at wine as something other than holy, a pleasure that's all too secular. David White brings wine back to its true place, a place the ancients understood far better than we. So open a bottle and open this book: it will open your soul."

-Jehon Grist, Ph.D. Executive Director, Lehrhaus Judaica

May the spirit within you grow as you sip these words

Sippin' on Top of the World

Toasting Good Times and Better Days

David White

David White
WineSpirit Institute
For the Study of Wine and Spirituality
www.winespirit.org

WingSpan Press

Requests for permission to make copies of any part of the work
should be mailed to:
WineSpirit
855 Bordeaux Way, Suite 100
Napa, CA 94558, USA

1. Wine   2. Viticulture   3. Spirituality
4. Toasts   5. Meditation 6. Inspirational Reading
7. Wisdom   8. Life Management

Cover Photo: Rays of Light by Scott Schrader
www.winevalleyphoto.com

ISBN: 978-1-59594-312-5

Library of Congress Control Number: 2009927352

For Sharon L Cohn, my treasured love
and best friend, in celebration of 30
years of memory-filled marriage

Table of Contents

Section III – **Toasting Good Times And Better Days**

Section VI – Harvesting Wisdom Of The Ages

Sippin' Foreword and Acknowledgments

Sippin' on Top of the World explores life meaning, by making connections between wine, grapes, vineyards, and vines, and all that is special, wondrous and precious about life and the people with whom we share our journeys.

Periodically, over three years, with occasional WineSpirit Advisory Board member contributions, I crafted more than 150 Sips of WineSpirit: insights and inspirations, many of them generated in conversations at potluck dinners or participatory seminars. A Sip of WineSpirit continues as a periodic e-mail, connecting insights from the world of wine with spirituality in daily life.

To make wine, many conditions have to go right: soil, air, rainfall, sunshine, fog, and other elements ... plus human partnership, tending to the process: planting, picking, crushing, barreling, bottling, distributing, and pouring, for toasting special times.

At WineSpirit gatherings, people share stories, life lessons, and truths. They share favorite bottles of wine, and winemakers offer their own creations.

Volunteers lead WineSpirit programs and seminars, often in teamwork, for example, Master of Wine Tim Hanni and Professor Liz Thach together leading a discussion on the genetics of wine tasting, and its impact on how you "taste" life — the genetics of preferences. Napa Valley College's Paul Wagner, who teaches Cultural History of Wine, volunteers his expertise in leading seminars on topics such as tracing the history of wine from Babylonia to James Bond, or the history of the banquet. And so that leadership goes: with scientist Dr. Sondra Barrett, wine and food editor Maria Binchet, winemaker Charlie Johnston, tour guide leader

Steven Russon, wine educator and sommelier Burke Owens, and others contributing in special ways.

Such partnership has produced *Sippin' on Top of the World*. Sonoma State University Wine Business Professor and WineSpirit Advisory Board member Liz Thach persistently encouraged me to publish the Sips of WineSpirit. A blessing I had not anticipated was Dr. Thach, with experience in self-publishing, actively partnering in the process.

WineSpirit Advisory Board members that contributed to *Sippin'* include Steven Russon, who created the book title, taken from the name of one of several of his Sips in this volume; Liz Thach, offering a poetic Sip; Paul Wagner, who helped develop WineSpirit programming, providing several Sips; Sondra Barrett, scientist, who discovered wine's mystical properties in the way it looks under a microscope, (www.sondrabarrett.com); and Larry Leigon, who has facilitated WineSpirit organizational development.

David Freed, WineSpirit Chairman, co-creator of WineSpirit, and my spiritual brother and dear friend who encouraged and enabled this publication, contributed editorial input, as did Elaine Freed, Paul Wagner, Sondra Barrett, Maria Binchet, Ray Mayeri, Steven Russon, and Liz Thach.

Betty Teller's assistance was invaluable in her thorough editing of the final manuscript and her outstanding suggestions for improvements in the content.

Paul Wagner crafted introductions to each section.

Special thanks go to my administrative partner, Waunice Orchid, and accounting manager, Kathy Archer, both of whom oversee WineSpirit day-to-day operations and who assisted with the logistics of publishing *Sippin'*.

Sippin' on Top of the World is dedicated to you, and to your friends, enjoying wine and spirituality: awareness and awe for that which you are thankful for ... special people, good times, and unusual circumstances ... spiritual access points, in the course of a day, to notice ... and engage.

Enjoy *Sippin'*, now ... and again ..., that your journey be rich in meaning and reward.

Cheers! To Life! Cin-Cin! All the best!

David White
Executive Director WineSpirit
Napa, California
April, 2009

Introduction

What is WineSpirit...Home to *Sippin' on Top of the World*?

WineSpirit is a blend of what is new and what is ancient. To explore the relationship and partnership of wine with spirituality is to connect with a 10,000 year-old agricultural product that offers insights gleaned over thousands of years: strategies for restoring balance in difficult times and perspectives on what and who are important and worthy of celebration and gratitude.

People around the world use wine, to pause and celebrate friendships, relationships, and enjoyment of fine food. WineSpirit celebrates all avenues that enable you to stop, now and again, to treasure such moments. Understanding wine and its spiritual and cultural underpinnings encourages different ways of reflecting on choices for breathing new life into set patterns and traditions.

What are WineSpirit's Origins?

WineSpirit began as a conversation between two Davids: a businessman and a member of the clergy. Both sought to integrate spirituality into the business of life: to create ongoing awareness and celebration of specialness in moments throughout each day. Without such integration, business and spiritual realms remain apart: isolated pieces, separate fragments in the course of a day.

After several years of searching for integration in addressing matters of life balance and fragmentation, the Davids realized that the business of grape growing and wine production often overshadowed the joy and blessing of turning grapes into wine. They perceived that religious institutions and organizations had many items on their agenda, with spirituality, but one among them.

From another perspective, they shared amazement over how many people were drawn to the vineyard as a calling, a special feeling for the grape and the magic that it produced, with the reward at the dinner table, crowned with a toast. They were not drawn to apples, bananas, berries or dates. They were drawn to vineyards.

The Davids perceived that from a spiritual perspective wine throughout time was the chosen means to fulfill an obligation of sanctifying particular occasions and events, to add meaning and significance to moments in the lives of individuals and groups.

As they shared questions and reflections with friends and colleagues, some of whom became WineSpirit Advisory Board members, what dawned on them was growing delight that, each time they conversed, they gleaned more insight into wine's extensive role in celebrating life and relationships. In applying wine metaphors, they blended knowledge with passion, identifying moments as special, even holy; they experienced those conversations, and all that they uncovered, as spiritual. With glasses raised they celebrated varieties of teachings, from widespread traditions, joining in alignment and in unity, in toasting life.

WineSpirit Institute was created as a 501 (c) (3) non-profit educational institute, for people to explore and share their stories, connecting wine and spirituality in the quality of the moment.

WineSpirit activity has included filming 11 Elders and Sages of the Wine community, and addressing how their work in the vineyard changed their lives. Among those interviewed: Brother Timothy, Robert Mondavi, Justin Meyer, Al Brounstein, Jan Shrem, Margaret Duckhorn, and Jamie Davies. (Contact execdir@winespirit.org for more information about which DVD's are now available)

WineSpirit focuses on spiritual and social benefits associated with wine and relationships. With a glass of wine, raised in a toast, one catches a precious moment and relationship, an act of priming the spiritual pump.

Sippin' on Top of the World is a collection of eighty-eight, from over one hundred and sixty, brief writings, distributed as an email series, titled *A Sip of WineSpirit*, generated, mostly, by Executive Director David White. The focus is on insights, shared over hours of conversation: lessons from the vineyard and life balance, vs. daily reality. Each Sip invites you to toast, now and again, what is good in life, and times and people that you treasure.

With *Sippin'*, accessible to the public, WineSpirit will extend its base, beyond the Napa Valley, and invite readers, through the website, www.winespirit.org to connect with each other: brainstorming insights, strategies and choices, to turn ordinary moments into extraordinary and memorable ones, in WineSpirit gatherings, in your homes and in your neighborhoods.

Enjoy *Sippin' on Top of the World*...and celebrate what is special about your life and the people with whom you share your journey.

Cheers! Salute! Cin Cin! Skaal! Prosit! To Your Health! Sante! Salud! Oogy Wawa! L'Chaim! To Life!

Sippin' Suggestions for Using the Book

PERSONAL REFLECTION: Set aside time in your day for *Sippin'* and reflection......with a glass of wine... savoring a Sip and the moment... stopping and noticing all that is good, and for which you feel gratitude

SHARE TOASTS: Enjoy *Sippin'* with friends during the evening... choosing favorite toasts, including *passages in bold italics*... wonderful for dinner parties and celebrations... toasting special times and memorable occasions

JOIN IN THE CONVERSATION: add to the *Sippin'* Reflection Questions, at the end of each Sip, and write a Sip of your own. Send your questions and Sip to execdir@winespirit. org, and we may include them in future editions.

ADD PERSPECTIVES ON WINE AND SPIRITUALITY: Engage a unique way to appreciate wine ... and spirituality ....*Sippin'* old traditions in new light... providing fresh perspectives on your religious, cultural and spiritual paths

GROUP DISCUSSION: Use for weekly, or monthly, discussion groups ... *Sippin'* wine and spirituality, in daily life...with friends and kindred spirits .... life's preciousness, shining through your life stories

WINESPIRIT GROUP ACTIVITY: Bring WineSpirit into your neighborhood ... *Sippin'*, while you share insights, at meetings, and blogging on the WineSpirit Website...

Breaking Down Barriers: Wine and Spirituality

It's not easy to contact our spiritual side... it seems that many elements of our busy lives conspire to prevent it.

But wine often helps to open those doors; it gives us reason to be thankful (and thoughtful) and creates a sense of communion among those who share it.

Ironically, wine, too, can be intimidating to some people. But wine should not be feared--it can be an important ally on the path to spirituality, and an avenue to the more important things in life.

Sip 1: Breaking Down Barriers: Wine and Spirituality

In choosing a gift of wine, are you sometimes overwhelmed by the number and variety of brands on the shelves? Do you find it easier to pick a six-pack of microbrew beer than a similarly priced bottle of wine? There is a mystique associated with wine that intimidates many people, who assume that only those steeped in wine culture can easily access it. The wine industry is challenged to find ways to make it simpler, easier and more inviting for people to buy wine.

Just as wine can seem inaccessible, so is it the case, for many people, with spirituality. Many are interested, but feel it is beyond reach. *The mystique of spirituality is intimidating.*

Wine and spirituality share important dimensions: There is no one way to experience a moment as uniquely special, as spiritual. And, there is no one way to enjoy wine. One person's ordinary wine is another's taste treat. One person's ordinary moment is another's extraordinary blessing.

As the wine world seeks different ways to make wine more accessible, especially for those presently choosing other libations, one way for that to happen would be to bring to light wine's age-old role in connecting people with spirituality. Understanding that role could encourage increased acknowledgment, celebration, and toasts to life's blessings.

You access spirituality by appreciating its function in this physical realm: to encourage you to use every opportunity to turn ordinary moments into special ones.

REFLECTION QUESTIONS FOR SIPPIN':

1. Which is more intimidating: choosing a wine or

seeking spirituality, and how has that changed for you over the years?

2. What obstacles do you face in accessing spirituality?

3. What could the wine industry do to attract consumers by connecting wine with spirituality?

4.

Sip 2: What Scales Do You Use to Evaluate Wine—and People?

Over 25 years ago, Robert Parker created a quality ranking system that made wine increasingly accessible to more people. His numbering system, now broadly applied, gives some consumers the confidence to make their choices. Parker's 100-point scale opened up the world of wine to those who, without that guidance, shied away from wine altogether.

Yet the scale reflects Parker's palate, not everyone—or anyone—else's. The apparent precision of the measurements and the impact of Parker's judgments on consumers' choices tempt winemakers to aim toward such standards, but his ratings can contradict the elusive, individual quality of wine. What is most important in a wine is whether you enjoy it.

Educators and executives seek effective and accurate ways to measure people and their abilities, achievements, and character. The 100-point grading system used in many schools is but one of many flawed assessment alternatives attempting to distinguish one person or group from another. What makes grading challenging is that people are unique. Precise measurement is not easy—if it is even possible.

Wines, like humanity, are multi-nuanced and difficult to define. Each wine, like each person, is unique, subject to change over a span of time. With so many to choose from, it is no wonder that we turn to measurements and standards to help make the selection process more tenable.

The human desire for a rating scale—and the reality that such scales are flawed— accentuate the human-like characteristics inherent in wine, reflecting life in all its complexity. Beyond generalities and numbers is the reality that what you have in your glass is unique: a combination of a particular moment, a friend with whom you share it, and the taste of the wine in that context.

Wine is not math. One person's grade of 83 may be another's 92, whether evaluating the same person or the same wine. That is what makes life, and enjoying it with a glass of wine, so special. You are right about what you are drinking — and Robert Parker is right, too. Yet your scores may be very different.

REFLECTION QUESTIONS FOR SIPPIN':

1. How much do you rely on expert input in selecting books, movies, wine, and other things?

2. How do you allow for human factors, variations, and flaws in choices you make?

3. What ways do you find most useful or rewarding to help you discover wines you love, and how do they compare to ways you evaluate people?

4.

(Inspired by W. R. Tish's Industry Forum: Wine Ratings 2 of 3, Wine Business Communications: 12/5/04)

Sip 3: When Does Your Opinion Count More than the Expert's?

An important principle in wine tasting is that your opinion matters more than the expert's. While many can agree on a great wine, there is always room for differing opinions. That is true with all wine.

Justin Meyer, founding co-partner and winemaker with Silver Oak Cellars, brought that point home in his comment about the 1986 Napa Cabernet Sauvignon. When they first started pouring it, he remembered, the public's response was different from what he had expected. He, the winemaker expert, did not have the highest opinion of that wine. It seemed too light to have the appeal for which Silver Oak was known and valued. The public disagreed. They tasted a wine that was rich and full of aging potential.

Time revealed the public was right. It ended up being one of Silver Oak's finer vintages. Justin realized that his knowledge and expertise as a winemaker did not make his opinion of the wine more valid than that of visitors to the tasting room. Even with his background and experience, he did not see and appreciate in his own wine what others had tasted.

It is humbling and empowering to keep in mind that no one, not even the winemaker, has exclusive expertise in matters of taste and preference.

Whether a winemaker or a visitor to the tasting room, for each, the tasting experience is unique and valid. In the case of the '86 Cabernet, the passage of time revealed that the consumer had a better sense of the wine's potential than even the winemaker.

REFLECTION QUESTIONS FOR SIPPIN':

1. In your area of expertise, how do others contribute in some way to your knowledge?

2. What goes into an expert like Justin Meyer yielding graciously to the wisdom of the layperson?

3. What is involved in your feeling comfortable and confident in choosing a wine?

4.

Sip 4: Who Knows Wine Better than a Sommelier?

A friend related that, to gain admission to a wine and food tasting in another state, a wine magazine editor friend arranged for him to be their representative. The hosts of the tasting asked him to be a wine judge. Determined to back out of the plan, he called his friend, who assured him he knew wine well enough, and gave him this advice: "Be true to your opinion."

With trepidation, he joined a team of two other judges. One was a local newspaper wine reviewer that he figured didn't know much more than he, given his own access to California wine. The other was a French sommelier.

Tasting the first wine, the sommelier was ecstatic: "This is one of the finest wines!" The pretender, not knowing what to say, suggested it was premature to give such accolades at the start of the tasting. The expert dismissed the next wine: "It's awful!" The pretender, angered from the start by the arrogance, despite his insecurities, blurted out, "I disagree. This is a wonderful wine!" The wine reviewer, also angry, agreed with him.

So it went a number of times: the expert pontificated, and the two spitefully disagreed. With the sixth tasting, the sommelier began to blurt, then stopped: "What do you think?" They gave their reviews, again in agreement with each other, and the sommelier agreed with them. So it went with each wine thereafter: harmonious reviews.

How fascinating that a wine judging became a study in people: their values, self-assurance, and the impact they had on each other. A professional wine person, wrapped up in his self-importance as a sommelier, was taken apart by two lesser credentialed people, put off by his overbearing arrogance.

How ironic that a tasting of wine, whose quality is

measured by its balance, could bring out such imbalance in people, in the ways they pass judgment on wine and one another.

However you read the experts, what is enduring is that wine engages each person's taste buds uniquely, making "experts" of us all.

REFLECTION QUESTIONS FOR SIPPIN':

1. How is it possible for an expert in a field to be unnerved by relative amateurs?

2. What do you make of this paradox: You can devote a career to understanding wine and its taste, yet each person's opinion is legitimate?

3. To what degree does your work expertise spill into other areas of your life, such as your sense of self-worth and self-esteem?

4.

(With thanks to Steve Arnold)

Sip 5: What Can Harley Davidson Teach the Wine Industry?

A representative of Harley Davidson gave a fascinating presentation at the 2004 annual meeting of WineVision, an American program for unifying the wine community. His message: motorcycles and wine have much in common. Harley wanted to overcome a bad guy image evoked by the Hells Angels and other tough guy imagery. They sought a way to make their product appealing and accessible to bankers, corporate types, and regular people ... you and me.

Wine has its own stereotypes to overcome. One, dating back to Prohibition, associates wine with other alcoholic products as an instrument of intoxication, as in "wino." Another connects it to European culture: wine drinkers are seen as snobs; fine wine is not for common folk who lack proper knowledge of its properties.

Harley's transformation of image involved a soul searching that evoked two important principles. First, they realized it is not about selling motorcycles, but lifestyle. On Saturday, bankers exchange suits for jeans and leather jackets and go out riding. They join fellow riders in weekend celebrations of freedom: an escape from the ordinary, from societal stereotypes, liberation from the rigid formality of dress and the rigors of daily schedules. That led to a second principle: individuality. Harley makes countless varieties and colors of bikes so that each owner can feel unique and special at rallies, gatherings, and biker conventions.

Parallels to wine are striking: *Wine is neither about intoxication nor snobbery. It brings to life moments to celebrate: times for happiness and joy ... opportunities to embrace dear ones and create lifetime memories. It is a unique 10,000-year-old gift, dedicated to sanctity of life.*

Its contribution: enhancement of food at a meal, enriched by people enjoying each other's company. Wine is about individuality of taste; each wine, unique among thousands, is special to those who enjoy it.

Ironically, Harley is further along than wine is in accomplishing its goal of convincing the public to see beyond tattoos and understand its contribution to enhancing quality of life. The wine community has much more work to do to overcome its stereotypes. It is a task that ought to be relatively easy, considering that, throughout history, wine's existence has been predicated on achieving and celebrating quality of life, both in secular and religious contexts.

REFLECTION QUESTIONS FOR SIPPIN':

1. **What parts of your lifestyle enhance and enrich your quality of life?**

2. **What examples beyond Harley and wine come to mind as programs and products contributing to quality of life?**

3. **What are other examples of stereotypes keeping you from better understanding and appreciating a person, a product, or a group?**

4.

Sip 6: A Lifetime of Grace
Bestowed in a Moment

WineSpirit's Paul Wagner shared a poignant moment in the life of a childhood sweetheart who was going through awful times with her mother. His friend was also recovering from the devastation of an abusive marriage. In an effort to provide a measure of comfort, Paul shipped her some wine.

Sometime after, she called to thank him and shared this story: She and her abusive parents had gone to counseling, where she tried to explain her pain. Her mother interrupted with details of the harm done to the mom by her own father. The mother could not see her own anger over how well her father had gotten along with his granddaughter. This caused much of the dysfunction. Both the counselor and their pastor urged Paul's friend to have very limited, but respectful, interactions with her parents, because they were incapable of any kind of meaningful relationship and would continue abusive patterns of conversation.

Out of fear, she had not spoken alone with her mother for three years, but she had brought her a Mother's Day card and flowers a few days earlier. On Sunday afternoon, she heard a quiet voice inside her head say: "Call your mom and wish her a happy Mother's Day." NO, she said to herself, to the voice, and argued that she had already done enough. The voice persisted. She called and was grateful her mother did not answer, so she left a message.

It was also Mother's Day for her, and she was alone in her big house, about to be sold. She felt resolution that day; somehow, the overwhelming problems weighing her down were slowly working themselves through. She opened the wine her friend Paul had sent and enjoyed sitting quietly, in a flow of spiritual calm. She was feeling wonderful and warm on this beautiful, sunshiny Mother's Day afternoon.

That evening, the phone rang. She was so relaxed that, this time only, she did not check caller ID to see who was calling; she just picked up the phone. It was her mom, calling to thank her for the kind message. In the afterglow of that afternoon, she found herself able to speak without fear and to listen without taking offense: "This is okay; that is who she is; let it go." After she hung up the phone, she laughed at how God had helped her to work through a huge fear and to begin breaking down a wall. Now, with deeper understanding of her mother, she realized that her words would never sting as much again. She also perceived God's sense of humor: the quiet and calm of slowly sipping a glass of wine had stretched her beyond her comfort zone. The following Sunday, her mother's birthday, she called again, this time without the aid of a glass of wine. It was hard, but she did it, smiling at God's tactics to get her where she needed to go.

REFLECTION QUESTIONS FOR SIPPIN':

1. How have you, or someone you know, had an unexpected breakthrough with a parent or other significant figure, and what factors contributed to it?

2. What was involved with this young woman's coming to grips with her mother's dysfunctional parenting?

3. How do wine and/or other ingredients of life factor into tackling difficult, if not impossible, situations and interactions?

4.

(With thanks to Paul Wagner and Cathy)

Sip 7: What Happens in Accessing Inner Beauty?

By Sondra Barrett

Do you look only at the surface of a person or the label on the bottle?

Do you use externals to tell you about the inner person or wine?

How often are you turned off by what someone looks like, never getting to know who that person is, what his or her soul is like?

I am part of a singing group, and one man in the group has a gruff voice, crooked teeth, and a poor-hippie look. He seemed very tough. When I would see him before we began singing together, I felt an immediate discomfort and dislike. I never wanted to engage him in conversation because of how he looked and seemed.

Yet over the months of communing with our voices, I discovered that this—to my eye— externally challenged individual is one of the sweetest, most spiritually balanced, and loving people. He is a true shaman/priest. And I missed out on months of enjoying him because of the external.

The same goes for choosing wine—I often let the label convince me that what's inside the bottle is good. Once I began looking at the inner wine through the microscope, I not only began enjoying wine more, I began seeing that the *inner wine* might be a more adequate way of labeling the bottle, to give us a glimpse of the real insides

My microscope reconnected me with spirit three decades ago when I first looked at living cells. Now once more it reconnects me with the sanctity of life in our everyday interactions with one another and while enjoying the occasional glass of wine.

For most of my adult life, I have been a health scientist and teacher talking about how best to take care of our hearts and cells. And research offered from medicine is finally beginning to recognize that it is our human interactions that may be the most important to our health and well-being.

REFLECTION QUESTIONS FOR SIPPIN':

1. What is it you do to create human connection?

2. Do you let the externals guide you?

3. Are you patient enough to get inside wine or a person's "soul?"

4.

Sip 8: How Could Wine Calm Your Mind and Open Your Spirit?

If you are in a hurry, you might order iced tea, bottled water, or a soft drink with your meal. When you want to slow down and enjoy a leisurely repast, you might order wine. Sipping wine can slow you down to help you relax and enjoy your meal and your dining companion.

Wine was part of the solution for one person, after she enrolled in an art course that forced her to "draw with the right side of her brain." The left side was analytical, she was told, and hers dominated and blocked her from drawing freely. Her instructor suggested that she have a glass of wine before coming the next time and she did. It resulted in better and freer drawings. So that is what she has done ever since.

All too often, you are in a hurry. You are late. You have to keep up, with so much to do. You can only see the broader picture of life when you are relaxed and reflective, open to imagination and intuition. Sometimes a glass of wine can help.

Wine's magic manifests in how it enhances food while helping people to connect. You drink it in sips, slowly and deliberately. Enjoyed in moderation, it slows you down and opens you up, elevating consciousness.

A glass of wine encourages you to gain perspective, while helping you restore balance and feelings of well-being. It makes sense!

REFLECTION QUESTIONS FOR SIPPIN':

1. What part does wine play in helping you relax?

Breaking Down Barriers: Wine and Spirituality

2. How do you permit yourself to stop what you are doing, to enjoy a glass of wine, lest you think of *stopping* as wasting time?

3. What benefits would you gain by tapping into such brain capacities as instinct, intuition, imagination, reason, and scrutiny?

4.

Sip 9: What Could Happen by Extending the Conversation?

Whenever you interact with someone, you have a choice: You can keep it brief or go deeper.

While vacationing in Vermont, we ate at a restaurant called The Garlic, where they served a lovely meal that included a practice worth replicating — a complimentary 2-ounce taste of a featured wine. As we finished, the server asked if the meal was to our liking. We started to give the usual reply, "Fine." But, for some reason, that night we went further. "You know what would have made this good meal better? More garlic!" That comment led to comparisons with The Stinking Rose, a restaurant in our area that features more than enough garlic for a garlic lover. As the conversation followed its course, we indicated that our last vacation stop, which was next, would be a rendezvous with family in Torrington, Connecticut. The server responded that she drove there every weekend to visit her boyfriend. That in turn led her to tell us what we were longing to know: the fastest, best, and prettiest route to Torrington. She was better than AAA.

Apart from the timing and synchronicity — how many towns are there in Connecticut? How many servers are in all the restaurants in that resort area and know as much about the town in question, let alone make the drive every week? — we realized that this exchange would not have happened had we not extended the conversation and commented on the food.

This was a delightful reminder that opportunities and choices to go further and deeper present themselves constantly, particularly in mundane daily interactions. As one server in Killington, Vermont, demonstrated, it could result in help from an unlikely source.

REFLECTION QUESTIONS FOR SIPPIN':

1. What does this Sip have to do with wine?

2. How have chance meetings had unexpected outcomes after you went deeper?

3. What impact have coincidences had on you and your life?

4.

Gleaning Lessons from the Vineyard

Our modern lives take us far from the earth, the soil, the sun, and even, at times, the sweat of our brow.

But wine is a product of a specific place, where soils, climate, and the hand of man all combine in a single bottle.

Wine plays a key role in connecting us to all of those things and the blessings they bring.

Sip 10: How Do Wines You Choose Reflect the Values You Live?

Attitudes about wine range from valuing it for its prestige to taking it for granted as you toss into your grocery cart an inexpensive red to enjoy with spaghetti. Choices in wine are as wide-ranging and varied as your moods in the course of a day. For some people, it is at times an expression of stature: pouring a prestigious wine on a special occasion. Others enjoy wine, costly or not, for its enhancement of a meal and an evening shared with family and friends.

How you value wine could mirror choices you make in life. Do material possessions accentuate and characterize who you are, or do they reflect the way you enjoy life, and how you share happy times? Or both? Perhaps, you sip wine as an experience to transform an otherwise ordinary day.

Wine's spiritual dimension comes alive in connecting people, filled with gratitude for daily blessings, with thankfulness for even common things and ordinary moments. It manifests in the awe of human partnership with nature and the blessings that abound in enjoying tasty wines.

Wine and its enjoyment are an expression of your lifestyle. Whether setting you apart or enhancing your relationships, it is unique as a beverage that helps you better appreciate yourself and who and what you value in your daily life.

REFLECTION QUESTIONS FOR SIPPIN':

1. What things in your life reflect who you are and your values?

2. How has your usage and appreciation of wine changed over time, and how does such change correlate with changes in yourself?

3.

Sip 11: How is a Vine Mightier than a Drill?

A winemaker pointed out that a vine is "stronger" than a steel drill. Over time, its roots can penetrate hard rock, in some ways more effectively than a drill. They spread in every direction, through every crevice, to reach life-sustaining water. The drill will get there faster, but only after breaking through the rock and disrupting the terrain, in contrast to the vine growing with the terrain. Metaphorically, the vine and the drill correlate with natural remedies and choices, contrasted with human-created solutions.

This lesson from the vineyard applies to the human condition. You might measure strength and power by weight and force pushing or pulling in desired directions. It is common to use powers of logic, experience, and authority to force outcomes. And when someone challenges your authority, you may feel like pushing harder. The vine's way of reaching the water implies that a greater power may be manifest in the planting of a seed, an idea, a thought, or an alternative. It may take stronger root and achieve a desired outcome more effectively than all the pushing and pulling that the strongest of people can generate.

There is so much more to reality that extends beyond the limits of human ingenuity. Nature's own remedies show alternate ways to tackle problems and, at times, achieve better results. You can see that with herbal remedies that complement Western medicine. You can see it through human partnership in tending the vineyard.

The partnership of human and nature, and lessons derived from that rhythm, could help with addressing societal ills, in generating creative strategies to achieve greater success in restoring health and balance to our world.

REFLECTION QUESTIONS FOR SIPPIN':

1. What are examples of illogical and unlikely solutions that are better than "tried and true" ones?

2. What steps can you take to become more open to alternatives to the way something is "supposed to be"?

3.

(With thanks to Charlie Johnston)

Sip 12: How are Wines and People Parallel in Mellowing with Age?

A friend shared insights accumulated over years of travel, while marketing wine throughout the world. He mused about the juxtaposition when tasting an older wine immediately after tasting two newly released vintages. The young ones were crisp, bold, and brash. The older was soft, subtle, and balanced.

He observed that many people prefer their wines younger. They seem more accessible. They are pleasing in color, fragrance, and the burst of flavor. Yet, he added, "Most young wines don't take you anywhere." A good older wine may not be as bright, as bold, or as powerful in flavor and composition, but there is a complexity of character, blended into a measure of balance, that only comes with age. It takes time to allow wine to age in the bottle, and then, as it is uncorked, the wine often goes through a process of opening up, as if to catch up with the years it was closed away in the darkness of the cellar.

He sees parallels between wine and people. Just as patience is a virtue that unlocks a fine old wine, so is patience a key to connecting with older people. It may be easier and more comfortable, especially for younger people, to connect with someone in their own age group. The expectations may seem more clearly defined. Yet, stories abound of young people connecting with older ones, whether within family or in some broader context. What begins as an awkward search to fill silence evolves into an interaction with surprising and rewarding results. All that was needed was time for the two to be with each other, to open up and breathe in the experience.

The interface of age and wisdom with youth is an important part of a process linking past and future. The past provides memories upon which to build new memories.

Toasting with an old bottle of wine could provide a catalyst for younger people to sit for a moment with those of a different age and outlook, and share tastes, attitudes, and values. It's a wonderful way to discover a new perspective.

REFLECTION QUESTIONS FOR SIPPIN':

1. What are your preferences for young and old: wine and people?

2. What are anecdotes that address relationships between young and old?

3. How have you changed as you have gotten older?

4.

(With thanks to Stephen Brauer)

Sip 13: How Does Wine in Moderation Help Restore Balance?

In the Bible, the first instance of intoxication is described with Noah planting a vineyard upon leaving the Ark. What did Noah know? As a novice, he could not have understood the importance of handling wine with care.

Reb Nachman, a Jewish Hasidic master, taught: "The entire world, life as we know it, is a very narrow bridge and the important operating principle is not to be afraid." The fear is of losing balance and falling off.

People often spend time out of balance, trying to keep up, while living with anxiety from unrelenting pressures.

A lesson from Noah's vineyard: Life is a balancing act. Drinking to excess dulls the senses, perhaps providing a moment's escape from life's pressures. Wine, while subject to misuse, is intended to serve a different function. It slows you down so that you can notice and appreciate connections: wine's enhancement of your meal, while enjoying family and friends.

Wine, in moderation, helps you relax, let your guard down, and enjoy doing so. Tasting wine, a sip at a time, helps you calm down and see more clearly the forest: the choices you make and how you live.

A glass of wine, gracing a meal, provides a wonderful setting for reducing stress and restoring balance.

REFLECTION QUESTIONS FOR SIPPIN':

1. How important is balance: In a wine? In your life?

2. What relationship do you see between moderation and balance, and what part does wine play?

3.

Sip 14: When Wine Goes In...
The Secret Goes Out

Judy, a visitor to a WineSpirit meeting, was impressed that the wine was accompanied not just by cheese and crackers, but by a level of discussion and dialogue that resulted in an outstanding experience of insight and sharing. Judy's contribution was noteworthy: "We all have our workaday roles that we play. They are usually identified as 'hats that we wear.' Yet, there is another part of us that is more about our heart, our feelings, and our vulnerabilities. Wine, as part of our meals, is a vehicle to opening up to that inner part of ourselves. In its proper usage we enable ourselves to transcend our workaday selves."

There is a teaching in the Talmud, the oral law of Judaism: "When wine goes in, the secret goes out." That can be either good or bad, depending on one's degree of respect for the power inherent in wine and its susceptibility to misuse. And the meaning of "secret" is broad. It includes what is going on inside you: emotions, feelings, and thoughts that you are more likely to access when you are calm and relaxed. A glass of wine in a setting with people you trust can enhance the experience, helping you let your hair down.

Judy caught the energy in the room, the power of the wine that encouraged free-flowing imagination as the group shared an hour of brainstorming about wine's relationship with spirituality.

As you appreciate the power of wine and enjoy it, you may allow "secrets" to come out, revealing truths and values that are sometimes difficult to access amidst the rush and crush of the day.

REFLECTION QUESTIONS FOR SIPPIN':

1. When is it good and/or bad that wine is conducive to letting secrets out?

2. What comes to mind of a special time with special people when secrets came out, and was it for good or not?

3. What role does moderation play in the conversation about secrets coming out?

4.

(With thanks to Judy du Monde)

Sip 15: How Could Cabernet Enhance Appreciation of Your Relationships?

What makes the most prominent of red wines, Cabernet Sauvignon, so magnificent is not only the care with which it is crafted, but often, the subtle blends of supporting wines that contribute to its greatness. A powerful Cabernet softens and becomes more accessible in partnership with Cabernet Franc, Merlot, and other softer reds. Different varieties of grapes, grown in different conditions and settings, are blended to create a wine of distinction and quality, greater than the wine each grape alone would produce.

When you reflect on shared associations while sipping a Cabernet blend, it could remind you of how your effectiveness is due, in some measure, to contributions of the others who work with you. Their strengths and characteristics are worth celebrating as part of your success. Those more forceful in their business dealings could pause to appreciate colleagues who are gentler and calmer in their ways; each contributes to the outcome. One person may stand out, yet everyone's contribution is valuable. Cabernet Franc and other grapes may only be a small part of the Cabernet Sauvignon blend, but together, the grape varieties create a fine wine. Pouring such wine is an opportunity to toast a blend of valuable relationships.

REFLECTION QUESTIONS FOR SIPPIN':

1. When do you notice and thank people who contribute to your success?

2. How do your relationships contribute to the quality of your work and home life?

3. How does your work add meaning to your life, even though someone else may get the glory?

4.

Sip 16: How Does Tending the Vineyard Extend to One Another?

Wine and people are a lot alike in benefiting from tender loving care. Making wine involves attention to the delicacy of the grapes and wine at every step of the way: planting, growing, harvesting, crushing, storing, bottling, and cellaring. If you are not careful with every facet, you risk diminishing the wine's quality, since it is a product of both the genetics of the grape and the environment in which it is grown, made, and protected.

People also benefit from tender loving care. Parents and teachers help children develop value and self-worth in the ways they give them encouragement to do and be their best. Adults accomplish more when they work in an environment of mutual respect and cooperation, with sensitivity for each other's particular quirks and characteristics.

How wonderful it is when the loving care that goes into making wine culminates in toasts celebrating life's wonderful relationships. This delicate fruit of a carefully tended vine comes alive through words and sips, as people treat each other with the kind of care and attention that produced the wine.

Sincere toasts and good wishes contribute to the quality of life: moments to savor in seeking blessings and well-being for those near and dear ... here and now.

REFLECTION QUESTIONS FOR SIPPIN':

1. What analogy could you make between the caring process of turning grapes into wine and its application in your life?

2. What parallels could you draw between how people treat plants and other forms of life, and their fellow humans?

3.

Sip 17: How Does Sustainability Extend from Vine to Glass?

One of the earliest adherents of "sustainability" — recycling as much of the harvest of nature as possible — was the wine industry of New Zealand, inspired by the pristine beauty of its unique and relatively isolated island nation. Since 1994, New Zealand wineries have moved in the direction of ecological balance in the interplay of working the soil and growing their wine grapes. Most New Zealand wine land is subject to sustainability regulations. The industry also encourages its members to keep such balance in the running of their businesses and in their financials.

You could also apply sustainability in personal and interpersonal ways: not only making a commitment to recycling, but also to taking time to regain your balance. Sustainability manifests in stopping for a moment, or a day, or a week: to relax, unwind, and be yourself — the self you would like to be — among those who share your journey. In stopping to relax and reflect, you allow yourself to consider all that you do: How much of it is important? Do you make time for what and whom you value? Such questions could help you examine and appreciate your life balance or what you would need to do to address well-being physically, spiritually, and emotionally.

A glass of wine, raised in a toast, provides an opportunity to regain your balance and connect good people, good times, and life's manifold blessings. Raising your glass invites you to notice and appreciate more: where you are, with whom, and all that is special and precious.

With a lot happening in your life, it can be difficult to practice personal and interpersonal sustainability. Under too much pressure, you can lose your balance. Toasting helps you savor a moment, and, in so doing, regain a measure of balance.

Sustainability is not just for wineries and vineyards; it's for everyone.

REFLECTION QUESTIONS FOR SIPPIN':

1. What connection do you make between sustainability of the land and in your life?

2. How might people who practice sustainability gain in productivity and success?

3. What impact could commitment to sustainability have on your work?

4.

Sip 18: What Contributes to Your Having a Good Day?

Wine growers know that producing wine involves complex relationships and interdependencies. For the wine to reach the marketplace, many things must go reasonably well: working the land, decisions about which grapes to grow, caring for the vines, the winemaking process, and the storage and aging facilities.

Each link is critical, including how the wine is stored and displayed once it gets to market. From planting to opening the bottle, every step involves coordination and cooperation.

Adding to the complexity are the myriad varietals and vintages of wines that winemakers produce and customers buy. Wine's variety and distinction mirrors such differences in people and the individual facets that have shaped our development over the years, contributing to who we are today.

While sipping your next glass of wine, you could reflect on the process it likely went through before reaching your dinner table. That, in turn, could remind you to appreciate more of what went well for you that day, and all that contributed along the way.

REFLECTION QUESTIONS FOR SIPPIN':

1. What factors are involved in the successes of your day?

2. How do you notice all that goes well without doing so only after something has gone wrong?

3.

Sip 19: How Does Wine Differ From Other Beverages Containing Alcohol?

By Steven Russon

Beer, wine, sake, and distilled liquors all contain alcohol, a compound with the power to physically affect the human body. Depending upon the individual and the amount ingested, alcohol can be a stimulant, a social lubricant, an inhibition release, a depressant, or, in extreme cases, a toxic substance.

So how is wine different from other beverages that contain alcohol? Grapevines, alone among fruits, seem to "know" why they are here on earth. They make and store unusually high levels of sugar in their berries. They produce an exceptionally high amount of juice per berry. They also secrete a waxy cuticle covering the skin of each berry that is a perfect medium for the spontaneous growth of living yeast cells. When ancient man collected ripe fruit and tried to store more than he could eat, most of it spoiled—but the grapes became wine.

A further difference lies in wine's direct connection with the yearly cycles of weather and harvest. The other beverages mentioned above are made from grain and can be brewed or distilled at any time of the year. Wine is made only at that one time of year when ripe fruit is harvested. Each vintage reflects, in its tastes and richness, a faithful diary of the climate and influences of the year when the grapes were picked. Where other beverages are formulaic, the same, batch after batch, much of the lasting allure of the wine experience is the way it changes from vintage to vintage,

Lastly, wine has a life in the bottle that parallels the cycles of other living things. It is awkward at first and must be sheltered. In the wine business, this is called "bottle shock."

Wine is typically held in warehouses for several months before release to allow this condition to settle. Then, upon release, its raw youth is observed, with forward fruit flavors and sometimes harsh tannins. With age, it begins to show more mature complexities, as new compounds are formed and short tannin molecules become longer chains, softer on the palate. Then, if stored correctly and protected from spoilage, the wine passes into middle age as the fruit begins to fade, and the subtle "bottle bouquet" develops. Finally, after a long life, it loses its fruit and dies, leaving only memories. Our task is to savor it for all that it shows us throughout the different phases of its life,

Wine is a metaphor for our lives and is uniquely suited to inclusion in our ceremonial or significant moments.

REFLECTION QUESTIONS FOR SIPPIN':

1. How do cycles of life flow through you?

2. Analogous to wine's uniqueness among alcoholic beverages, what distinctions can you draw between life conditions that are cyclical and those that are not?

3. What does wine's dimension as a *living* entity contribute to understanding and appreciating facets of human life?

4.

Sip 20: Where is the Balance between Constancy and Change?

You may find comfort in knowing that much of your life is predictable: how you handle your daily hygiene, your schedules, and other patterns that make one day similar to the next. Life can seem rich and full when your ongoing activity also allows time for spontaneous moments and unexpected adventures that keep you feeling vibrant and energized.

However you may feel about change and facing the unknown, one of the characteristics of wine is in not knowing its taste until after your first sip. Even with subsequent sips, you may detect subtle or blatant changes in taste. Wine awakens your senses, in accentuating that life includes spontaneity, change, and uncertainty.

A glass of wine invites you to celebrate life's less predictable facets and blessings that accompany you, in the constancy of change, hidden in life's repetitious moments.

REFLECTION QUESTIONS FOR SIPPIN':

1. **How do you balance predictability and constancy with spontaneity and surprise?**

2. **When is change your friend, and when not?**

3.

Sip 21: How Do You Balance What is Old and New?

Switching to a new computer reminds you that what is new becomes old very quickly. It is easy to dismiss anything that isn't current as out-of-date, irrelevant, and even useless.

It is difficult to reconcile the old and the new. On one hand, you may feel set in your ways; on the other hand, you may delight in the newest products and updates and quickly discard what they replace.

Wine is part of a world that blends old and new. While some lack patience to let a full-bodied red wine mature in the bottle for a few years, others appreciate the aging process, at least as it pertains to wine.

While grape growers will plant new vines, either to change varietals or to respond to diseases that attack the vineyard, they also maintain prized old vines, with their history of yielding outstanding vintages.

Whatever your attitude about aging, wine is one entity that can improve with age and is valued because of its association with tradition and with special years in which it was grown and harvested.

A lesson from the vineyard: life at its fullest includes old and new. "Out with the old and in with the new" is not the way of the vine. A nice aged wine beckons you to set aside time to enjoy it, savor it, and to toast the blessings of what is old along with what is new, in your ongoing life journeys.

REFLECTION QUESTIONS FOR SIPPIN':

1. How does your balancing of old and new play out in foods you eat and beverages you drink?

2. How have you changed, or not, over the years, in terms of preferences for old and new?

3.

Sip 22: How Does Passion for Quality Bring out the Soul in Wine?

Wine is a product of soil, grapes, growing conditions, winemaker, blending, aging, and for the consumer, cellaring and storage. Each step involves conscientious care to assure the quality of the wine.

The consumer chooses the right bottle that will enhance the taste of the meal and the quality of the time and moments to be shared.

Enjoyment of wine is qualitative: wine is conducive to sipping slowly and occasionally, during a gently paced hour or two.

Such appreciation of quality characterizes wine's association with spirituality: a blending of special moments and people sharing them. What is common and ordinary becomes memorable and treasurable.

Those who value wine for more than just its taste understand that quality extends beyond making a wine attractive to the market. Quality is a constant every step of the way, from planting to enjoying the last sip.

That last sip culminates a couple of memorable hours, spirituality manifested in bringing out the best in everything and everyone.

REFLECTION QUESTIONS FOR SIPPIN':

1. How does consciousness of quality affect your choices of activities and time you spend with people?

2. How do quality moments affect you in the moments after? A day after?

3. Does it help or hinder your connection to spirituality to think of it as thankfulness during quality moments?

4.

Sip 23: What Brings out Your Passion?

Silver Oak Cellars founder Justin Meyers said in a WineSpirit Video Conversation (one of the Spiritual Harvest Series), that he did his work with passion, and that it was wonderful to access that drive and power within. For him, it was a passion for the world of grapes, vineyards, and wine, an integral part of life.

For someone driven that way, making wine is more than a business. No part of it is easy, especially in difficult times, yet what transcends the stresses and difficulties is the knowledge that from start to finish you are dealing effectively with two special facets of life: vulnerabilities and successes.

Passion in the vineyard, and in tasting wine, awakens your spirit to the joys of life and the enjoyment of sharing good times and so many blessings with someone special.

While few can work and walk in a vineyard, on occasion you could make time to find a quiet place, a still space, for a breather — a break to ponder the lessons a vineyard teaches, and to reconnect with what brings out your passion. It may seem a difficult assignment, in the crush of a daily schedule, but in doing so, you could tap into energy within that might stir an awakening to appreciate and celebrate under-noticed blessings. You could also focus on what you love: activities, hobbies, friends, and places that energize you.

A passionate moment, filled with love for life, is one worth celebrating, not just in heartfelt toasts over special wines, but at any time you can pause to notice what and who matters in making life precious. Such moments allow bad things to become bearable and good things to become wonderful.

Gleaning Lessons from the Vineyard

REFLECTION QUESTIONS FOR SIPPIN':

1. What makes you passionate?

2. What are the positives and what are the negatives that you associate with passion?

3. How does passion awakened in you affect other facets of your day and your equilibrium?

4.

Sip 24: What Lessons of the Vineyard Could You Apply in Daily Life?

In the vineyard, vines yield grapes that, through the magic of human intervention, turn into wine. Each moment of the process is filled with the potential to make or do something good.

It is no surprise that grapes and wine, from antiquity, serve as symbols and agents for noticing life's blessings and celebrating them. The fruit of the vine contains what is *divine*, magical moments, little things that have to go right, to turn that grape into a special sip of wine. From ancient times, to our own days, lessons abound.

How many grapes go into a bottle of wine? Many thousands and more. They demonstrate that living alone, standing alone, and going it alone is not nature's way. When everything and everyone are in tandem, goals are achieved in collaboration. Each grape is a reminder that many facets go into a single achievement, a moment worth cherishing. As surely as all those grapes will be consumed as a glass of wine, savored for the moment, so each particular triumph passes, leaving you to anticipate the next celebration and accomplishment.

Vineyard teachings apply in daily life. You could choose to harvest the vineyard of your life, the seemingly ordinary moments ... sequences in ordinary days ... and transform them into extraordinary ones, filling every day with quality and outstanding achievements.

As lessons of the vineyard abound, so do possibilities to access countless extraordinary moments in many kinds of ways. Each of us grapes has a lot to contribute, after all, to the fruitfulness and blessings, the seeds and blossoms, that grow and flow through all of us and our individual journeys.

REFLECTION QUESTIONS FOR SIPPIN':

1. How could you liken your life to a vineyard?

2. What "lessons from the vineyard" have the most meaning for you and your living situation?

3. What example comes to mind of combined effort leading to significant accomplishment?

4.

Sip 25: What is Your Best Time of Day ... or Night?

Grape growers and winemakers know that time of day matters in picking grapes in order to catch the full character of the fruit as it begins its journey of fermentation into wine. In vineyards, where it is hot during the day and cool at night, it is desirable to pick the fruit after dark or early in the morning.

One particular benefit: the grapes are more balanced, in terms of sugar and acidity. In the heat of the day, the sugar level is higher than at night. It is desirable as well to pick when grapes are cool, and thus easier to handle.

The fluctuations and ramifications that pertain to picking grapes could also apply to people. You may notice fluctuations and variations in your own rhythm in the course of 24 hours. Some are night people, others morning people. Blood pressure also fluctuates depending on time of day and activity.

This "lesson from the vineyard" suggests a strategy for approaching the heat of a moment, when you are upset, or interacting with someone who is. Often, in moments of anger, words are exchanged, making difficult situations worse.

A way to repair the damage and restore some balance to the relationship would be to sit down and talk when tempers are cool and emotions are calm. You will likely hear each other better and accomplish more.

Choosing your times to act, and interact, could generate increased awareness of life's broader rhythm and ongoing fluctuations, each and every day.

Grapes, picked at night, begin a journey destined — months and years later — to yield a balanced wine for you to enjoy in harmonious moments: celebrating life's good and happy times.

Picking grapes or picking moments ... the trick is finding

better times to pick and choose, and to reflect with questions like these:

REFLECTION QUESTIONS FOR SIPPIN':

1. How do you tap into your best stuff at the best times?

2. When do you go easy on yourself and others?

3. What strategies help you reduce stress, relax, and enjoy the moment?

4.

Sip 26: How Do You Handle Ups and Downs of Holiday Cheer?

Christmas time can be one of mixed emotions. Those who have suffered a loss may find their joy tinged with sadness; a dear one and friend is missing from the festivities.

The December and January holidays are filled with parties, gifts, and cups of good cheer. How ironic, how stressful it can be to party and celebrate when you have other pieces of life weighing you down. The challenge is for happiness and joy to prevail over the stress and tension that many feel during the holiday season.

A lesson from the vineyard, as a measure of comfort: Unlike great cheese, which the California dairy industry touts comes from happy cows, wine can actually benefit from less-than-happy conditions. Many grape growers will tell you that grapes *stressed* with less irrigation, or thin, rocky soil, or by clinging to a hillside, will tend to yield more complex fruit, resulting in better wine.

You learn a lot about yourself and your capacities when you see what you can do and how you function under pressure.

Of course, *just as winemakers handle stressed grapes with great care in making wine, such is true, even more so, with people, who need support and nurture in times of stress.*

Whatever pressures or anxieties you may be feeling at a time of giving, sharing, and joy, you can lighten your load by remembering you are not alone. When you are caught up in trying to do the holiday right, remember that we are all in this together.

REFLECTION QUESTIONS FOR SIPPIN':

1. What comes to mind when you reflect on personal growth and success generated during a period of stress?

2. What factors are involved in your experiencing ups and downs at holiday time?

3. How could remembering growth's partnership with stress help when you are feeling anxious?

4.

Sip 27: How Does the Human Touch Bring Out Nature's Best?

Human inventiveness has enhanced certain foods and taste treats over the years. Filtered coffee is one example, juicers are another. Clos Pegase winemaker Shaun Richardson shared an example of human enhancements in grape growing to explain the value of estate-bottled wines.

"Back in the early 1970s at Chateau Petrus, Christian Mouiex walked out into his vineyard one fine July morning and started to do a very strange thing. At this time of year, the unripe green berries were beginning to change to purple, the step known as veraison. M. Mouiex believed there was too much fruit on the vine that season; if left alone, it would not achieve peak ripeness. He reasoned that if he removed some of the clusters, the vines would have more energy to mature the remaining crop. He then proceeded to cut a few clusters off each vine. Such a technique was unheard of at the time. He was dropping money on the ground, or, more outrageously, as the local pastor pointed out to the congregation the next Sunday, he was destroying God's handiwork!

"A grapevine is psychologically quite simple: if it is dark all the time, it thinks it is in the forest and it must produce more shoots and leaves to reach the sunlight. If the days are sunny, it thinks that producing all those shoots has worked well to get it to the top of the trees, and thus it should spend more energy on setting fruit so the birds will come and eat the grapes and spread the seeds (in individual "fertilizer packets"). The vine's behavior can be measured in the field by the Leaf Area to Fruit Weight ratio (LA:FW), which compares the weight of the vine pruning to the weight of the crop for the same season.

"If the LA:FW ratio is too high (such as in a forest), the vine regulates its hormone levels to produce more vegetative growth, to seek the sunlight. A low LA:FW ratio means that the vine may not be able to photosynthesize enough sugar and flavor for fully ripe grapes ..."

This gleaning of the behavior of a vine only came to light after someone had the imagination and courage to go counter to common wisdom and prune measurable profits in exchange for immeasurable gains in quality, well worth its weight in reputation.

Parallels in the human condition are worth musing about over a glass of wine.

REFLECTION QUESTIONS FOR SIPPIN':

1. How do you make the hard choices?

2. When do you dare to follow your instincts?

3. What do you prune from your life?

4. What do you anticipate as consequences of your actions?

5.

(With thanks to Jan Shrem and Shaun Richardson)

Toasting Good Times and Better Days

Wine is more than a beverage; it can also sometimes be a key part of a ceremony or ritual: a marker of important occasions, a time to reflect on what has gone before, and a chance to ask for a blessing for the future.

Sip 28: How Can Raising Your Glass Elevate a Moment?

Toasting with wine is a unique ceremony, transforming the ordinary into something extraordinary. Toasting does, in secular contexts, what religion does in sacred settings. One of religion's goals is to teach and evoke awareness of life's ongoing blessings and of how special each day is. Wine can evoke a similar feeling each time you open a bottle and share a glass. You toast and make the moment special, possibly memorable.

At the table, wine serves the dual roles of enhancing the taste of the meal and the character of the moment. In cultures around the world, the words and gestures are different, yet the sentiments are alike: wishes for better health, success, and enjoyment of the moment and beyond.

Schmoozing over a glass of wine in the warmth of a toast is spiritual, as it connects people. Both through religious ritual and the clinking of glasses, opportunities abound to identify and celebrate special moments ... to savor and cherish, and add to your treasury of wonderful memories, immortalizing the best of life.

Time moves swiftly. Seasons fly, leaving you to wonder how, where, and why, so much went by, so fast.

Each glass of wine raised in a toast presents an opportunity — to catch rays of light, joyous memories, times shared with good people, and blessings embedded in each new day. It offers time dedicated to reflection, appreciation, and renewal.

REFLECTION QUESTIONS FOR SIPPIN':

1. How could seeking opportunities to toast enhance your quality of life?

2. What are ways that you draw nearer to people?

3. How could you slow time down, with what benefit?

4. What do you know of different cultures' uses of wine in ceremonial ways, and for what purposes?

5.

Sip 29: When Does a Glass in Hand Evoke Gratitude?

In religious and spiritual traditions, rituals and ceremonies remind you of details of life, often overlooked: miracles of all that goes well.

People commonly forget to tell others of their love, affection, respect, or gratitude, so easily taken for granted. Ritual and ceremony provide antidotes. They enable you to keep alert to life's ongoing blessings.

The key is to *stop*. In stopping, you can look around and see others and their contributions to your success, and you can give thanks for your associations and relationships. In the crush of a work day, it is as easy to lose sight of higher principles as it is difficult to let go of irritations and disappointments.

The challenge is to find moments to catch up, to raise your glass and toast. Both religious traditions and secular mores evoke gratitude: for those you are with and for what you are sharing. Toasting provides a context to answer the reflection questions that follow, and so many other ritual questions.

REFLECTION QUESTIONS FOR SIPPIN':

1. What gratitude is in your heart ... for God, for life, for love, and for friendships?

2. How could you schedule more time for stopping to toast life and those around you?

3. How do you give higher priority to *stopping*?

4.

Sip 30: How Does Wine Contribute as a Wellness Medicine?

Doctors and patients have traditionally measured health in terms of physical symptoms: You went to doctors for tangible ailments. In recent times, an alternative approach to medicine has emerged, focusing on wellness and preventative measures for maintaining good health. Awareness continues to grow that matters of attitude — mental, emotional, and spiritual — also contribute to physical health.

Multiple studies indicate that, for many people, moderate consumption of alcoholic beverages can be beneficial to their health. Increasingly, people associate consuming moderate amounts of wine with physical and emotional well-being.

Minimizing stressful conditions and not pushing daily activities beyond healthy limits are part of wellness medicine's agenda. Stopping with family, friends, and associates to enjoy a glass of wine and camaraderie provides a means of stress reduction, adding spiritual benefits in the feelings of relaxation and calm.

Whether expressed religiously or culturally, each time you raise a glass of wine and look in another's eyes to wish him or her well, you are introducing into your day an activity that promotes wellness, balance, and good health. It enhances your physical disposition, even as it gives you a moment to pause, breathe in life's blessings, and appreciate all that is going well in times of good health and well-being.

REFLECTION QUESTIONS FOR SIPPIN':

1. How have you adapted your lifestyle to wellness medicine?

2. How has sharing a glass of wine contributed to your sense of wellness?

3. What other measures could you take in support of preventive medicine?

4.

Sip 31: How Does Your Cup Overflow with Life?

In welcoming the Jewish celebration of the Sabbath with a blessing over wine, some people pour the wine to the top of the glass. What spills onto the table symbolizes the blessing of abundance, compensating for any concern over the stained tablecloth.

In the biblical days of Solomon's Temple in Jerusalem, High Priests offered special gifts to the Divine and poured wine on the altar. As they began to pour, other priests sounded horns, representing joy, and the Levites, extended family of the priestly tribe, sang. All the people were uplifted with joy and thanksgiving. It was a treasured moment, drawing near to the Source of Life.

Beginning any meal with the pouring of wine could become your own ritual, toasting relationships and celebrating abundance. With cups overflowing, you consecrate your table with songs of life, tales of times gone by, and memories warming your hearts. Raising your cup of joy could link you with the past and with those who have helped shape your life story. These are offerings of nearness and dearness, one with another, deepening and broadening relationships, partnerships, and friendships.

Pouring wine and sharing sips invite people to open up and to enjoy special relationships, growing richer and more precious with each sip of wine and life ... tastes to savor, often and always.

REFLECTION QUESTIONS FOR SIPPIN':

1. **What are special times that bring you close to family and friends?**

2. What rituals do you have: special traditions, unique ways to share blessings with others?

3.

Sip 32: When Do Words Mean More than You Say?

My son once asked, after sneezing, why the response: "Bless you"? It is one of those rote responses in life, whose meaning has been lost in its frequent utterance. So much has disappeared in the commonness of rituals that abound in society. "Goodbye" has long ceased to mean: "God be with ye." Raising your wine glass and making a toast can be pro forma rather than tasteful and heartfelt.

When done with mindfulness, blessing someone who sneezes connects vulnerability with thankfulness for good health, and with people caring for one another. Parting with "goodbye" invokes God's presence to be with people you wish well, an added blessing, to accompany them along their day's journey.

Of all the rituals permeating life, toasting with wine has the potential to awaken people. You look each other in the eye, you speak words that fit the occasion, and in that instant nothing else matters but that special exchange.

Blessings are easily forgotten, and their powers diminished, in the perfunctory ways people say the words, "Have a good day." Raising a glass of wine to mindfully toast with the fruit of di-vine could reawaken you to all that is precious and extraordinary in life ... so much, and so many people, for which to give thanks and sing praises.

REFLECTION QUESTIONS FOR SIPPIN':

1. Does repetition have to dull the senses?

2. What happens when you are mindful of blessings you bring others, and those coming your way?

3. How could you succeed in actually having a good day when someone wishes you one?

4. What could you do to better absorb blessings coming your way in the course of your day?

5.

Sip 33: A Toast that Went Round the World

With the birth of a baby boy, a father welcomed extended family for a special visit with mother and newborn in their home in a small town in Israel. He toasted the guests with a bottle of wine he had been given by his uncle at the end of a visit in Napa a month before the baby was conceived. He reflected on his uncle and aunt and their encouragement of family and friends to celebrate special times together.

In toasting, the father said he had been saving this bottle for a special occasion, and today seemed to be the right one. Opening it in celebration of new life took him back to Napa, to memories from that visit and values shared. He appreciated his uncle's and aunt's wisdom, and their teaching that family is important, as is celebrating special times. In sharing his words, he felt his Napa family's presence, with spirit abounding, in wonderful ways.

When the newborn's great-uncle, WineSpirit chairman David Freed, read these sentiments via email, he wrote back: "It reflected, in yet another light, that wine is a way to mark time and capture memories."

A toast in a small town in Israel went round the world, as a Napa wine was shared in celebration of new life and the promise of many more moments awaiting family celebration. The newborn is beginning his journey in a world considerably smaller than it was when his grandparents and great-uncles and great-aunts were born.

The proud grandfather, basking in his son's toast, observed: "The one bottle of wine was enough for more than 20 people to enjoy, and, like magic, it seemed to appropriately fill each glass. Not so many liquids can be spread so thin yet be so full."

The proud great-uncle in Napa added, "You give new meaning to the concept of sharing a bottle of wine. And, to think, wine came from the earth in Napa and ended up being transported and consumed in the holy land of Israel, at a special place and time. No other food or beverage has quite the potential."

REFLECTION QUESTIONS FOR SIPPIN':

1. **What story do you have of a bottle of wine, with a beginning (when it was acquired) and an end (when it was consumed)?**

2. **When has a celebration and toast made you mindful of people who are with you in spirit, though removed in time or distance?**

3. **When did a particular bottle of wine, opened for a special occasion, add depth and meaning beyond its taste?**

4.

(With thanks to David Freed, in celebration of the birth of Elad Tal)

Sip 34: How Could the Holiday Spirit Be with You All Year?

Thanksgiving Day is every day for those who give thanks at every opportunity. December, Christmas time, is designated for happiness, festivity, and consciousness of blessings: sharing them with each other and giving particular attention to the poor. People are more conscious between Thanksgiving and New Year's to add a little something for those who are in need.

The challenge is to find a way to keep this frame of mind and attitude when you resume your regular life in January, after the holiday season. Whatever is worth reflecting on during a particular holiday—such as a cup of good cheer at Christmas—is also worthy of sharing throughout the year.

Wine's history is as a beverage of consciousness. Its purpose and function, from antiquity forward, has been to help us celebrate and appreciate life.

In Christianity and Judaism, wine connects you with God. From Christian and Jewish perspectives, your gifts, talents, and resources are God-given, not for self-indulgence but for your own use and to benefit others. Embrace that, and the holiday spirit will live within you, and in your actions, every day.

Each moment is an opportunity to fill with blessing or to squander as mundane. Seasonal holidays shine festive light on how wonderful it is to bring good doings and best wishes into everyday life.

Life the way it is—with people on their better behavior primarily at designated times—does not have to remain the way of the world. *In toasting the best in life, you could also reflect on changes that would make the close of the holiday* season, and the start of the New Year, a real beginning, to assure that holiday blessings abound throughout the year.

One constant to apply in the coming year, and ever after, is to associate your toasts with the cup of good cheer. Recall, in those moments, that needs addressed at holiday time don't disappear with budbreak in spring.

REFLECTION QUESTIONS FOR SIPPIN':

1. How do you integrate values worthy of December celebrations into your everyday consciousness?

2. How do you address poverty and those in desperate straits every day, as an individual, a family, and a community?

3. How much is your toasting like the greeting, "Have a nice day," said by rote as a societal custom, lacking thought and feeling?

4.

Sip 35: How Can Each Day Be a Holiday and a Memorable Day?

The course of a year includes many holidays, some shared as a nation, others through the particular faith traditions to which different people belong. You may value some more than others. Mother's Day seems to draw more attention than Father's Day, and Memorial Day more than Veteran's Day. The ways you observe special days, or not, reflect your values; some matter to us more than others, some, not at all.

There is so much more to celebrate and appreciate than what is addressed in mandated days of observance. These official days could serve as reminders to notice what they commemorate every day; to appreciate more of life's ordinary blessings. That could increase focus on mothers and fathers. It could mean gifts of flowers, chocolate, and wine for loved ones more often. It adds mindfulness of Memorial Day and Veterans Day every day, with awareness of those who serve our country and safeguard its freedom. The Fourth of July could inspire a daily exercise in counting blessings of this country, its unique vision of rights for everyone to live in freedom and dignity, and the happiness of a society that celebrates differences.

The toast accompanying a meal is its own reminder that every day contains holiday-type elements, worth noticing and worthy of celebrating.

REFLECTION QUESTIONS FOR SIPPIN':

1. How many holidays, small and large, are worthy of celebration ... today?

2. How about creating new personal holidays, for example, Brother's Day or Sister's Day?

3. When, if ever, do you remind yourself, "Today is the first day of the rest of your life"?

4.

Sip 36: How Do You Catch Time in a Bottle?

The Bible mentions seven fruits of the Holy Land: wheat, barley, fig, pomegranate, olive, honey, and grape.

The grape, rendered into wine, attracts attention in a variety of ways: its history, geography, and the human involvement in making it into wine. Changing year after year and bottle after bottle, wine takes on its own life. Each bottle is a time capsule, holding a unique story.

Those knowing wine well may remember each particular year and how the elements shaped the character of that year's wines. Opening up a bottle that ties to a particular celebration, such as a birthday, an anniversary, or another milestone, unites past and present, spanning from the year the wine was made to the present.

None of the other biblical fruits offers this ability to span years, to change with our lives, maturing and aging alongside us.

Like the rings of a tree, telling tales of the past, the taste and character of wine bring forth stories of earlier times, from its beginnings as a fruit on the vine. Each is unique to the year, the vineyard, the winemaker, and the way it was handled and stored. *The tree tells its story, after it is cut down. A bottle of wine also carries a story — a precious few of them even spanning the years of a human life — that it shares when it is opened and drunk.*

Capturing the past, and tasting it in the present, reflects spiritual living. It raises consciousness, linking toasts and tastes, celebrating then and now, and moments of joy and appreciation for so many of life's beautiful and bountiful gifts.

Toasting Good Times and Better Days

REFLECTION QUESTIONS FOR SIPPIN':

1. What life stories and experiences are worth sharing over a glass of wine?

2. What are memories of *then* enriching *now*?

3.

Sip 37: Where Were You When ...?

Americans will long remember the inauguration of Barack Obama as the 44th president of the United States, just as many still recall the additional month it took to determine who was elected president in 2000. These are unforgettable memories, events not likely to happen again.

Ironically, it often takes an extraordinary experience to make a time in life truly memorable. Lacking such moments, life's repetitive nature lets days slip by, unnoticed and undervalued.

Weeks go by. Where did the year go? What can you do to slow it down? Does it require a crisis, or a once-in-a-lifetime event, to enable you to experience a day or week you will actually remember?

Those who enjoy a glass of wine hold in their hand one response to this riddle. Whether in religious and spiritual traditions, or in secular and cultural milieus, wine throughout the ages has been partner to opportunities for turning moments in any day, especially mealtime, into something special and memorable. Wine has ingredients that complement a meal and your enjoyment.

The key is your consciousness in the moment. *Focus on the ritual: hold the glass, raise it, share a toast, clink, taste, and savor. These all contribute to feeling the preciousness of this particular time together, in all its facets.*

What separates you from having another forgettable meal, a piece of an ordinary day, is the mindfulness and concentration you bring to what you are doing and those you are with. The fruit of the vine is an agent of awakening, a reminder to open your senses to this moment. This time will not come along again in just this way.

REFLECTION QUESTIONS FOR SIPPIN':

1. What does it take for you to notice and reflect on an ordinary day going well?

2. What unique traumas and awakenings have you had that resulted in no longer taking something or someone for granted?

3.

Sip 38: How Do You Celebrate Spring's Promise of Renewal?

The wine world has a wonderful holiday of spring, celebrated on different days in the spring season, depending on terroir and growing conditions: budbreak, when new growth emerges from the vines. As a Napa Valley newspaper heralded, "Budbreak is here. Let's count our blessings and lift our glass to a new season of cheer!"

Spring is a time of renewal, of opportunities to celebrate new possibilities, to elevate life and rejoice in all we have.

The Christian community during this season welcomes Easter, opening up to deeper renewed relationships with the Power that gives life and love. In the Jewish community Passover commemorates release from all kinds of enslavement beyond the physical — to time and scheduling, to ideas (because "that's the way it's done"), or to money — all symbolized by escaping from "Egypt," which in Hebrew means "constriction".

There are so many ways to celebrate this season of life, love, and freedom to begin anew: the Easter Feast, the Passover Seder, the rejoicing in budbreak.

The Seder, with its four glasses of wine that accompany a festive meal and the telling of a story, has its parallel in every occasion where people gather for an evening of fine dining and fellowship. The enjoyment of a multi-course meal might include pairing wines with different courses. Changes in tastes of food and wine blend with the ebb and flow of conversation.

Whether it be a vintner's dinner, business people celebrating the close of an arduous deal, couples celebrating their anniversary, winegrowers rejoicing in budbreak, or folks enjoying a special meal to welcome spring, these festive banquets and feasts become significant events to savor and cherish as you bask in the warmth and glow of renewal and welcome the lighter time of year.

What a wonderful season, filled with renewal, rebirth, new light, renewed hopes, optimism, and the joy and blessing of freedom. Choose to notice and celebrate spring and the fruits thereof.

May the growing light of this time of year add spring to your steps, and may all your glasses be full and overflowing with the blessings of renewal and the planting of seeds that will yield wonderful harvests in all that awaits you, as the year continues to unfold.

REFLECTION QUESTIONS FOR SIPPIN':

1. Which is your favorite season, and what makes it special?

2. What special seasonal activity do you enjoy, particularly in spring?

3. How does understanding the life cycle of the vineyard contribute to your awareness and appreciation of the cycles of the year?

4.

Sip 39: When is it Good to Go Home Again?

If you find you are spending more time with family and friends, and entertaining more at home, you are not alone. In years of economic downturn, increasing numbers of people do more at home, spend less on possessions and concentrate more on time with friends and family. Home entertaining can cost less, and it feels good. Relaxing over a meal is not just enjoyable; it also nourishes your appetite for more good times, making wonderful memories to enjoy and celebrate.

Since September 11, 2001, many people have determined to treasure today, since tomorrow—even later today—is an uncertainty. Staying at home and inviting others in, more than any time since the 1950s, has led to enhanced enjoyment of today's blessings: wonderful moments at more affordable prices.

For each celebration, there are wines to choose, balanced in taste, character, and price. Good wine, a good meal, and good people ... what blessings to come home to, and so much to toast!

Wine is good medicine for reducing life's stresses. The prescription: "Raise your glass; look into each other's eyes and toast. Cheers! To Health! To Life! Taste and share the joy and love in your hearts."

How good life can be, back at home!

REFLECTION QUESTIONS FOR SIPPIN':

1. How, if at all, have your habits, patterns, and usage of time changed in the years since September 11, 2001?

2. What has increasing awareness of life's fragility and unpredictability done to your priorities?

3. Do you have memories of a lovely and leisurely meal that provided an oasis from pressures outside?

4.

Sip 40: Does a Toast Make You Feel Included or Excluded?

By Larry Leigon

In a CD by Tom Harpur, author of The Spirituality of Wine, Harpur suggested that certain people have a problem with toasts, feeling that toasting one individual, as at a wedding, raises one person above the rest of us.

I suppose there will always be people who don't agree with me, but it seems to me when we celebrate an individual through a simple ritual like the toast we always have the choice to notice again that the individual is part of us, that we really are all in this together, and that to toast one of us is to toast all of us.

As for factors that include or separate, elevate or diminish ... it seems to me that any ritual, from the smallest to the largest, has to deal with the problem of trying to define and capture something that can't be defined or captured. It doesn't matter whether it's a small private ritual by a single person to honor a birth or a death, or the inauguration of the president of the United States, or the Christmas Mass at the Vatican.

For the ritual to be alive, it must somehow touch in us something greater than ourselves, something in which all of us are together. It must bring into awareness some experience, however small or fleeting, of that connection to everything that is not-me, or it is empty.

All too often, it means nothing at all, or it honors those being toasted as if they had created their own talent or skill — and in that case folks who have problems with toasts are right. The toast is saying that one person is above us all. More insidiously, it says unconsciously that our own personalities are more important than whatever it is that makes us alive in the first place.

The difference in meaning, it seems to me, must lie somewhere in the area of intention, of the ability and willingness to be present, of sincerity, and of a conscious decision about what we are honoring ... ourselves, or that which is greater than us. Whether the lifting of the glass means anything or not depends on us and our willingness to at least entertain the possibility that we are not the source of what we think or do.

Hosts and hostesses of gatherings and parties can better set the tone for the event in those they invite and how they make them feel at home. When guests feel they belong in the gathering, more likely a toast for the "honoree" will elevate the entire group assembled.

REFLECTION QUESTIONS FOR SIPPIN':

1. As host, what steps could you take to assure that all of your guests feel included and connected at the party?

2. What factors contributed to your feeling put off by a toast for an honoree whom you like and respect?

3. What example comes to mind of the elevation of an individual that uplifted all attendees?

4.

Sip 41: How Did an After-Dinner Toast Create a Life Memory?

By Paul Wagner

I have been invited to a few important dinners in the Factory House in Porto—the heart of the Port wine trade and a sort of exclusive gentlemen's club for major Port wine producers. The dinners are always delicious and elegant; after dinner, as you might expect, the whole group moves to another lovely room where we enjoy a fine glass of vintage port.

But one dinner there will always stand out in my mind.

The meal was hosted by George Sandeman, the seventh generation of his family in the wine business. After we had all been served our Port (from the 1956 vintage, as I recall!), George asked us to do him a favor, and he rose to offer a toast. He told us that his father had passed away just a few hours earlier, after a long illness, and he asked us to join him in raising our glasses to a fine gentleman who would never again raise a glass in the Factory House that he loved.

It was a very moving moment, and we were all deeply honored that George would include us in his toast.

REFLECTION QUESTIONS FOR SIPPIN':

1. What do we share when we raise glasses together?

2. How does a toast create a kind of communion for those who participate?

3.

Sip 42: How Did a Wedding Toast Turn Loss into Joy?

Family and friends gathered for a wedding that brought celebration into the lives of people who, almost two years earlier, had confronted the death of the 34-year-old sister of the groom. Jessica had lost a battle she fought her entire life, against the ravages and complications associated with Juvenile Rheumatoid Arthritis.

Two years later, the dominant mood shifted, from shock and sadness to joy and celebration, over the marriage of Jessica's brother to the woman his sister had enthusiastically welcomed into his life, before her death. But could Jessica's presence be acknowledged during the wedding without diminishing their happiness? A candle in her favorite color, purple, was lit under the wedding canopy, along with mention made of her and other deceased relatives in the program.

At the rehearsal dinner, people took turns toasting the couple. As each toast was made, two of Jessica's friends began to feel that something was missing. After all, Jessica was the big sister, who, two years earlier, gave her blessing to her brother and encouraged him to marry this wonderful woman. Surely she belonged at the festivities in a more direct way. As if propelled by some greater force, quite spontaneously they included Jessica in their toast. They said how pleased she was about this special couple, and how much she would want the room to be filled with delight and joy in celebrating them.

The effect of the toast was palpable. Everyone breathed a sigh of relief that turned to unbridled joy. They now felt Jessica's presence, filling them all with happiness. The toast by her friends replaced shadow with bright light that warmed every heart. Clinking glasses and sipping wine in Jessica's honor gave everyone permission to let loose and join with this family in joyful celebration. As one guest commented to Jessica's parents, she had never seen such happiness at a wedding before.

What a blessing is the ritual of toasting, providing a format for people to add to and enhance the joy of all assembled. It took that ritual, in that context, to enable a bride and groom and their family and friends to come out from the shadow of life's painful realities and bask in the glow of a new and wonderful reality, an uplifting memory for the ages.

REFLECTION QUESTIONS FOR SIPPIN':

1. In addition to toasting, what structures and contexts encourage broad and deep participation and sharing?

2. What is it about a toast that can change the energy in a room, in a significant way?

3. What do you recall of a time of great joy bringing healing to a memory of sadness?

4.

(In Memory of Jessica Saal)

Savoring Life's Blessings

Is wine proof, as Benjamin Franklin said, that God loves us and wants to see us happy?

A glass of wine is a kind of Sabbath — a chance to withdraw from the daily cares and worries of the world and focus on those greater issues that can so easily disappear, slipping through our fingers.

Here is a toast to what really matters.

Sip 43: How Does Tasting Wine Enhance Tastes of Life?

Wine tasting does not start with the tongue. It engages all the senses, and more — imagination, awareness, and openness. It begins with sight: seeing the label, the shape of the bottle, the color of the wine, the way it clings to the glass. Then there is sound: hearing the popping of a cork, the splash of wine in the glass, and the clinking of a toast. Smell is intimately connected to taste, as you sniff and notice the wine's bouquet and search for descriptors that recall fruit, flowers, spices, and other memories. The sense of touch is engaged as you note the wine's texture and viscosity inside your mouth, and as you swallow.

And of course it is above all about the sense of taste, from the initial sip through to the finish.

Throughout, if you are tasting with others, there is also a thread of communication, as you share notes and reactions each step of the way.

The ritual of wine tasting demonstrates that life is full of opportunities to taste more than just what the tongue brings to awareness. In life we often do everyday things mindlessly, based on previous experience and paths. Most interactions would benefit from taking a wine tasting approach, using all the senses. *Fruits of life come in many flavors. They are ever-present to enjoy, if you notice them and take advantage of the moment.*

You can apply all the nuances of wine tasting — increasing awareness in interacting with people — in other parts of your life. Tasting wine with all your senses could serve as the model for a more rewarding way and means to experience life as a taste treat.

REFLECTION QUESTIONS FOR SIPPIN':

1. What are your tastiest treats?

2. What or who could help you taste and savor more of life?

3. How does tasting good food and wine affect you inside?

4.

Sip 44: What is Special about Opening Wine?

There is something ritual-like in removing the cork from a bottle of wine. Ritual enables people to connect with years and generations past, recalling and reflecting how things have always been done, in this case, for a few hundred years.

Wine's antiquity — it was the first agricultural product mentioned in the Bible, with Noah planting his vineyard — bears testimony to its unique place as an agent for celebrating life.

When you mindfully apply ritual, you focus on the purpose and meaning of what you are doing, which you otherwise might approach mindlessly and unconsciously, having done it so many times before. It brings the moment alive; it links past generations to what is happening now.

Wine provides special tastes of life, beginning with the ritual of removing the cork, an obstacle in the path of enjoyment, a reminder, that success does not tend to come without problems. Bits of cork in a bottle remind you that things don't always go perfectly well.

And as you increasingly choose bottles with screw tops, it reminds you that times change, inviting new possibilities and contexts for new rituals for celebrating and sanctifying life.

Enjoying wine and the people with whom you share it allows what goes well to counter what does not. You keep your balance, as tastes of wine and stories shared transcend other difficulties, at least for the moment.

REFLECTION QUESTIONS FOR SIPPIN':

1. What rituals enhance your life and elevate your consciousness?

2. What rituals help you remember to appreciate life's challenges, obstacles, and blessings?

3. Are you better off with a screw top?

4.

Sip 45: How Could Eating Slowly Be a Diet for Healthier Living?

Americans, reportedly, struggle more with their weight than do the French. Mireille Guiliano, author of a unique approach to weight loss, *French Women Don't Get Fat: the Secret of Eating for Pleasure,* suggests why. Many Americans eat like robots, or on autopilot. It's not like eating. It's like stuffing yourself; you can't taste most of the food, because your taste buds are only on your tongue.

Guiliano's advice basically comes down to this: Eat only good food. Relax, and savor every bite. French women eat with all five senses, allowing less to seem like more. When Guiliano is with friends, in Paris, even if they are just eating sandwiches, they sit down, take their time, look at the sandwich, and admire the bread or the butter on it. They eat slowly. They chew well. They stop between bites.

Much has been written, in recent years, about the French paradox: People drink lots of wine and eat baguettes and high-fat foods such as creamy sauces, red meat, butter, and cheese, yet they still stay slim and have less heart disease. But it's not such a paradox. Will Clower, author of *The Fat Fallacy: the French Diet Secrets to Permanent Weight Loss,* says the French eat real food, not faux foods, like chips, sodas, Fruit Roll-ups, and cheddar Goldfish. They eat a wide variety of fresh foods, including plenty of fruits and vegetables, but not a lot at one sitting. They value quality over quantity.

Many Americans are fed up with keeping running calorie or carbohydrate calculations on every bite they put in their mouths; the idea of losing weight by eating well is seductive.

These are the strategies French women use to maintain their weight: Consume three good meals a day, watch portions, eat lots of fruits and vegetables, use seasonings, eat a variety of seasonal foods, drink plenty of water, savor wine, walk everywhere, including up and down the stairs, and indulge in a treat every once in a while.

When you slow down, with smaller bites, you savor food more and you are satisfied with less. After some time, you could notice some differences: Your palate will change and so will the way you look at food and portions.

Slowing down and being in the moment, often and always, is the path of spirituality; to see it in light of healthier living and greater enjoyment will yield the fruits of spirituality.

REFLECTION QUESTIONS FOR SIPPIN':

1. How does weight factor into your state of balance in the course of a day or a week?

2. What impact do these assertions of weight control among French women have on you?

3. What does it take for you to understand that slowing down or stopping is not *down* time?

4.

(Synopsizing Nanci Hellmich, USA TODAY, Jan 3, 2005)

Sip 46: What Wines Contribute to Great Memories?

By Steven Russon

I have worked in and around the wine business for more than 25 years. This has afforded me the opportunity to taste far more than my share of the world's finest wines.

Many of my friends and associates have been equally blessed with similar experiences. In such circles, when some specific wine is mentioned, someone usually recalls tasting it and, in true wine geek fashion, is only too glad to professionally describe every nuance.

Often, however, those same conversations arrive at the perennial question, "What is your most lasting wine memory?" Invariably, rather than just a description of the attributes of the wine, the answer paints a picture of the place, the circumstances, and the company.

Often, in fact, the wine turns out to be some unnamed local libation shared on a romantic evening at a beautiful beach or in a similar scenario.

It is clear that to enjoy a joyful, fully engaged life, one must look farther than just things, no matter how highly rated they are.

REFLECTION QUESTIONS FOR SIPPIN':

Take a few moments now to recall three of your favorite memories:

1. What, if any, are their common denominators?

2. Are the things that make you the happiest a part of your everyday life?

3. If not, what can you do to make them a part of that life?

4. How can you strive to create great memories every day?

5.

Savoring Life's Blessings

Sip 47: How Can You Turn a Bad Experience into a Good Memory?

How remarkable it is, when a tale comes to light as a result of timing and coincidence. Vintner Margaret Duckhorn gave most of a September day to the Wine Industry Symposium, held annually, in Napa. She ended the first day of that two-day program at the Master Sommelier Dinner, which gathered people from throughout the world at Groth winery. There, she was seated next to a woman from the East Coast. The woman told this story:

Some years ago, she was in Russia for her studies. In general, she found daily living in Russia depressing. She did all her studying in a tiny room. When depression began to hit harder due to weather, job, and missing family time and the enjoyment of sharing wine and a meal, she would go to her room, close her eyes, and visualize this experience: sitting there and tasting, once again, Duckhorn '84 Three Palms Merlot. It was eerie, because sitting still with her eyes closed, she could taste the wine: its richness and magnificence. It was real. Experiencing that wine in the fullness of her imagination became a powerful meditation, relieving her from stress and pressures and giving her strength to confront her tests and tasks. This meditation moved her out of her funk every time. And every time she now tasted the wine for real, it was eerie – a very good eerie.

This tale only came to light because of a confluence of disparate factors in Margaret's schedule. The dinner took place during a break in the two-day symposium. That is of consequence, in that it brought her back the next morning to a place where she could, so soon after, share the story with someone who would appreciate it. Margaret knew that David Freed, co-host of the Symposium, was also Chairman of WineSpirit, which treasures such stories of wine's contribution to the enhancement of daily living conditions, as an example of spirituality. And how, again, did it just so happen that out of hundreds of people at the dinner, Margaret sat next to one with such a story of her wine!?

REFLECTION QUESTIONS FOR SIPPIN':

1. Ah, coincidences! Had any lately? What can you make of it/them?

2. What memory do you have of food or wine as source of comfort, strength, meditation, and uplift?

3. What memory have you recently created that you intend to treasure?

4.

Sip 48: When Sharing Wine Calmed Nerves in a Time of Danger

In a WineSpirit program for the Napa Valley Tour Guide Guild, a participant shared a memory of wine helping to calm frightened people during a frightening time. She grew up in Denmark during World War II, and recalled the day it was announced that all Danish Jews had to surrender to the Nazi authorities. Her family was among many Danes who united in doing what they could to rescue Jewish neighbors. They went into the streets to invite any Jews they could find to surreptitiously come home with them.

As a number of people gathered under her family's roof, the tension in the room was palpable, with an air of unspeakable danger. Her mother, sizing up the overcrowded house, responded: "I'll just add a little more water to the soup!" The assembled guests gathered around the relatively undersized table for dinner, in an atmosphere heavy with fear and foreboding.

The mood only changed markedly for the better when her mother opened some of their finest wine and formally welcomed the guests. She never forgot how the weight was lifted, as people smiled for the first time, even laughed, in exchanging toasts, clinking glasses, and uttering hopes that this harrowing time would soon pass.

After the opening of that special wine, the evening took on an air of calm, even a measure of happiness. As it turns out, that bottle would contain a lifetime memory, of a historically horrible circumstance transformed into hope that all was not lost. It served as a symbol that there were yet good people with whom to harvest good times in an often unfriendly world.

A story such as this could serve as a reminder to hold onto good moments, good tidings, and well-being, and that, with each other's help, there are ways of coping even under the worst of conditions.

REFLECTION QUESTIONS FOR SIPPIN':

1. What factors enabled everyone to lighten up at that Danish dinner table?

2. What symbol(s) could you think of that remind(s) you of a significant, possibly life-transforming, time in your past?

3. What memory do you have of a special wine that energized a room?

4.

(With thanks to Elsebeth)

Sip 49: How Full is Your Cup of Life?

In the rush and crush of each day, it might be difficult to find time to pause and ask, "What is good about this day?"—to find something worth noticing, if you had a moment to do so.

As you sip wine while enjoying a meal, each sip provides a moment to pause, an opportunity to tap into feelings and thoughts.

How many sips are in your glass? How many moments of consciousness, of appreciation for good tastes—for the company you keep and the food you eat—are connected to the many sips that come out of that glass?

Sipping wine's spiritual dimension is a tasting of abundance: blessings, seeing the good even in hard times; it is recalling what goes well, more than what does not. It is acknowledging strengths you find in yourself to face difficulties, and enjoying feelings of triumph in overcoming obstacles.

What happiness to raise glasses, overflowing with abundance and gratitude! Each sip could help you refocus on positives that could counteract aches, pains, and disappointments that could pull your spirits down.

Each time you pick up a wine glass provides another opportunity to elevate a moment and dedicate it to more that is good, now and again.

I raise my glass to you, that in your life you find many blessings, even as you share them with others. To Life! Cheers!

REFLECTION QUESTIONS FOR SIPPIN':

1. What added strength could you gain by dedicating a

sip to something positive, to someone's well-being, in uttering a toast?

2. How many toasts are overflowing in your glass of wine?

3.

Sip 50: How Could You Have Your Vacation and Keep It Too?

A vacation—a change in scenery and a disruption of routine—provides opportunities to awaken you to dimensions of life often lost in the crush of daily activity. Going places, especially, for the first time, offers moments that could touch your heart and soul.

What fun it is to bring back tastes of good times, and to extend the vacation at home.

One year, we held onto a visit to Hawaii with tastes of Kona coffee. Another year, we returned with maple candies, syrups, and cheddar cheeses from Vermont.

Visitors to the wine country often bring home bottles of wine, reminding them of what they enjoyed in tasting rooms.

While Kona coffee, maple candy, and cheese have limited shelf lives, many wines could last for years and thus serve as unique time capsules. Opening them provides opportunities to revisit delightful memories while you are creating new ones.

A glass of wine with family and friends is one of life's little pleasures, a reminder to extend the joy and beauty of a vacation beyond summer and throughout the year.

REFLECTION QUESTIONS FOR SIPPIN':

1. **What positive effects does a vacation have on you, after your return?**

2. **What do souvenirs contribute to extending the magic of a vacation experience?**

3. **How does a day of wine tasting seem like vacation,**

and how did you recall it, some time later, when opening a bottle you had brought home?

4.

Sip 51: What Turns Ordinary into Extraordinary?

At a WineSpirit holiday party, people shared memories of special times and particular wines that accompanied those moments. I shared the memory of our realtor, bringing a bottle of wine with a swan on the label, in celebration of closing escrow on our first home. That ordinary wine had an extraordinary taste as we toasted our new home.

As people shared anecdotes, we learned that on many special occasions, a less than special wine had been part of the experience—and although it was more ordinary than not, the wine was remembered with fondness.

Extraordinary moments are not necessarily comprised of extraordinary ingredients. The act of toasting was what made a particular bottle special, more than the taste.

What is special and spiritual could manifest in a variety of ways, yielding a blend of the ordinary and the memorable that makes an experience extraordinary.

REFLECTION QUESTIONS FOR SIPPIN':

1. What story do you have of an ordinary wine that was part of a memorable experience?

2. Reflecting on something special that happened, what are some of the ingredients that contributed?

3.

Sip 52: I Am the Wine

By Liz Thach

Wine is a gift
from me   to you;
To help you relax
and feel me;
To sense the softness of my breath
     on the breeze,
To see the light in my eyes
     in the sunset;
To know that every
     tree, plant, flower, and vine
     blesses you   with positive energy.
I am the wine;
     I am the light;   I am life;
I am God –
     in whatever name
     you call me.
I am here.
     you only need to
     feel me –
     in prayer, meditation   in silence, in exercise,
     or in wine.
But
     not too much,
     not too little;
Just enough
     to ignite your heart
to touch the
     universal spirit around you.
Connect with
     your essence --
Which is me –

the world, the universe,
every atom of every
tree, blade of grass,
bubble of air.
I am Everywhere.
  I am You.
  You are Me.
We are Whole.
Join me
  in joyous celebration   of life,
      of now, of past, of future
of Being.
Thanks and gratitude
  ten thousand fold,   for this Moment!

REFLECTION QUESTIONS FOR SIPPIN':

1. **Which wine are you?**

2. **What, if any, memories does the flow of this poem evoke?**

3. **How is wine like poetry?**

4.

Sip 53: How is Life's Delicate Nature Reflected in a Wine Glass?

In conversation, a man indicated that in the past he used to drink wine, but in recent years he has chosen beer instead. On occasion, he said, he had had problems with wine—or rather, with the wine glass. More than once he set his glass down so hard that it broke. So now he prefers beer in a strong, stout mug or in its bottle.

While this motivation for changing beverages might seem quirky, it draws attention to a unique characteristic of wine. Wine is associated with life's delicate aspects. It gently influences the quality of a meal in the way it is paired with any variety of cuisine; it helps people relax; it inclines them to open up with each other and communicate.

How appropriate that wine is traditionally consumed in a glass with a broad base, rising up on a narrow stem, and then opening upward to contain the wine. A wine glass is delicate and fragile. Its shape parallels the transformation of grapes, which start out spread broadly throughout the vineyard, then go through the narrow confinement of the barrel and the bottle, and end up filling the glass—a happy ending—for celebration of life's blessings.

Many people enhance their enjoyment of wine with rituals and customs, treating the wine and the situation with dignity and respect, while enjoying the wine in moderation. Handling the glass with care is a tactile experience. It goes nicely with being at ease with people, sharing in the wine, and in the ambiance. *Everything associated with wine and the context in which it is consumed is indicative of treating life with gentleness and patience.*

Wine glasses also remind you, through their varying sizes

and shapes designed for different wines, that life is filled with details and nuances to attend to, or not.

It's nice to have a glass of wine in hand to calm you and energize you at the same time, as you take a moment's pause to relax and reflect and, at times, catch your bearings.

Then, again, if you are not inclined to tune into the subtleties and complexities of a moment with good food, good wine, and good people, there is always an alternative: Open a bottle of beer and veg out.

REFLECTION QUESTIONS FOR SIPPIN':

1. If you drink beer at times, and wine at other times, what conditions influence your choice?

2. How much, if at all, does the wine glass contribute or detract from your enjoyment of wine?

3. When are you more or less conscious of the supporting cast and factors that contribute to the success of a special experience?

4.

Sip 54: How is Body Language Relevant in Wine and in People?

In June 2005, Eric Asimov, wine editor of the New York Times, wrote in his column that there is a whole dimension of wine that is overlooked and underappreciated: wine's feel in your mouth. What is called "mouth feel" is an important contributor to the overall wine experience. Asimov indicates that the wine world has not developed adequate language to capture the feel of wine in the mouth, let alone the connection between its feel and the overall tasting experience.

A wine's mouth feel is important in enticing you to take the next sip. Its feel is the context for all the other elements of taste and enjoyment.

This overlooked facet of wine appreciation has a parallel in the human experience. Only in recent years has research indicated that communication is not as much the words used, nor the way they are used, but the total affect: how the person *is* in the interaction.

Communication mavens claim that in a personal interchange, what is said accounts for only about 10 %; the way it is said, 30 %; and body language, 60 %. Without seeing each other, we lose the subtlety and nuance of the interchange.

With our modern dependence on e-mail, text messaging, and phone calls instead of face-to-face interaction, it is understandable that breakdowns in communication could happen; there is too much emphasis on words and not enough on heart and soul, the way and being of the person, that tells you much more than what you hear or see on first glance.

With wine, if you don't take the time to feel the wine in your mouth—to let it sit there and engage you—you could miss an important element of what the wine is "communicating,"

In life, there is much more to tastes and quality than what meets the eye. A glass of wine, helping you relax, could enhance your next interaction with a family member, friend, or co-worker. Notice the body language, the feel of the wine, and enjoy the fullness of the experience and the interchange.

REFLECTION QUESTIONS FOR SIPPIN':

1. What example comes to mind of body language communicating differently than words expressed?

2. What facets of the tasting experience do you emphasize most in evaluating a wine?

3. Has "mouth feel" been one of those aspects to which you have given your attention?

4. What analogy could you make between noticing how wine feels and how a person seems in your interaction?

5.

*(Inspired by **The Pour: Wines Have Feelings, Too**, By Eric Asimov, New York Times June 22, 2005)*

Sip 55: How is Wine Unique Brain Food?

There are reports from Great Britain and France that, taken together, position wine as a unique food, particularly good for the brain.

The French wine industry, concerned about an increased harvest coupled with decline in consumption at home and in the export market, lobbied their government to redefine wine as a food. The claim: Wine provides sustenance as a food, and in moderation it is good for you. The proposal was in response to tighter DUI laws, credited with reducing traffic fatalities, but also resulting in decreased wine consumption in France. Classifying wine as food would allow advertising of wine without the restrictions applied broadly to alcohol.

Meanwhile, in Britain, a study was published by University College, London, in January 2004, indicating that as many as two glasses of wine per day, especially, for women, enhances brain function and thought processes as compared to teetotalers.

The study in Britain and the lobbying in France accentuate that there is something unusual and special about wine, more than just its enhancement of the quality of a meal. In both these cases, the stress was on wine in moderation. Wine in some ways has an inherent standard for moderation, in that drinking to excess ruins otherwise special experiences with food and people.

The principle of moderation applies to most facets of life. Life is contextualized by the truth that there can indeed be too much of a good thing. Given that life has physical boundaries and limitations, wine, like any product in this world, has its value and place in the big picture, when enjoyed within limits. Consumed in moderation, it associates with blessings that manifest beyond many boundaries.

The British study of wine's contribution to healthier brain

function supports the French effort to redefine wine as food, with its nutrients and benefits. *It all adds up to the enjoyment of a product that exists in order to remind us that life abounds with blessings to be enjoyed in this realm of physicality associated with our sojourn on this planet. To enjoy wine responsibly is in itself a reminder to live responsibly in everything you do. To live that way is to demonstrate how much better off we all are when we use our brains to do what is right and good, in all facets of our day.*

REFLECTION QUESTIONS FOR SIPPIN':

1. What serves for you as a reminder to live responsibly, in moderation?

2. What is your favorite association with wine?

3. What is an example of too much of a good thing, and the consequences?

4.

Sip 56: How Do You Go with the Spirit of *Flow*?

From the moment grapes are crushed, they flow, starting as juice in the barrel and ending as wine, flowing a sip at a time into your mouth and on inside.

The juice in the barrel matures, developing its character as wine. Eventually, it flows into bottles, where it continues to age until it is opened.

Finally, it flows into a glass, in readiness for enjoyment with food and people.

At last, the wine moves on to its final destination, the mouth of a whole new world where multiple senses come alive, uniting tastes and smells and sights, all part of the joy of life, a special moment, a memory in the making.

From crush to sipping, this particular flow of life gives pause. Savoring the wine and the people you toast, you are enjoying one of life's finer moments: the coming together of good food, good people, and good wine. That is the spirituality that makes life, and the flow of life, a constant blessing, worthy of all the toasts you share.

REFLECTION QUESTIONS FOR SIPPIN':

1. What part does enjoyment of wine play in the flow of your life?

2. Analogous to wine's transformation from juice to taste treat, where has the flow of your life brought you?

3. How does pausing to reflect on wine's odyssey add to the quality of the moment you are in?

4.

Savoring Life's Blessings

Finding Spirituality in the Details of the Day

God is in the details. And each day brings a new opportunity to notice the little things that matter ... An elderly couple holding hands as they talk ... A drop of dew in the morning sun ... A glass of wine shared between good friends.

Sip 57: Sippin' on Top of the World

By Steven Russon

In my youth I was half of a nationally known rock climbing team. I was, I confess, by far the lesser half—my climbing partner, Peter, being as close to Spiderman as I have known. The night before a climb, it was our ritual to open a nice bottle of wine with dinner around the campfire, reserving half to share on the summit the following day.

No other experience I have known has compared with rock climbing for achieving a sense of oneness with Mother Earth. One surrenders life and limb, trusting to her support and one's own meager abilities. Life becomes simple, more focused; the physical body is taxed nearly to the limit. At the summit, we relaxed. We would toast the climb and that sense of connection would expand. Our informal little ritual helped to slow the moment and expand it to a meditation.

Sadly, there seems to be a lack of similar ritual in our lives today. There is certainly no lack of repetition; even our constant barrage of entertainments is repetitive, but few of them offer us an opportunity for reflection.

By contrast, each morning when first seeing that the sun has come up, what a great moment it is to stop and think, "I've just witnessed a miracle ... again." Consider what would happen if it had failed to come up. Or more to the point, what would not happen.

Each new day, each moment, is a precious gift. The very presence of the sun each morning provides the venue for all of the other "important" things that may fill the rest of your day. The rituals we choose to observe within that day can provide each of us with opportunities to stop and reflect on the nature of things around us. If we choose not to observe, we give up those opportunities. Without reflection we are simple agents of reaction to outside stimulus.

REFLECTION QUESTIONS FOR SIPPIN':

1. What guides you to focus your thoughts on your connection to nature and our planet?

2. Are there any ritual elements you could employ that might help to sharpen that focus?

3. Can you devise a way to elevate some daily event to the level of a significant ritual that helps you to reflect upon some deeper meaning in your life?

4.

Sip 58: What about TeaSpirit, BreadSpirit and Olive OilSpirit?

Occasionally, people question the notion that wine, as a consumable, has a unique connection to spirituality. Those familiar with the Tea Ceremony appreciate its special, even spiritual, qualities. Home-baked loaves and artisan breads evoke in some people a special spirit, an elevated awareness of human connection with the earth and its bounty. Cooking with olive oil accentuates a special quality of meal preparation with an ancient ingredient. Varieties of bottled spring waters evoke in some an awareness of life's preciousness and its sources. Many people could not start their day without CoffeeSpirit.

To connect with and enjoy these other tastes of life in such special ways is an essential goal of WineSpirit. *Throughout its history, wine has provided an access point to spirituality: an opportunity to notice and celebrate particular moments and blessings of life. With tea, bread, coffee, and so many other special taste treats, you are also given opportunities to notice and appreciate life's little blessings and even miracles. What sets wine apart from all these, and from other special fruits, is that wine alone has existed from the start in a variety of cultures as a beverage whose purpose is to see, acknowledge, and enjoy life's precious moments, whether in religious settings or in otherwise ordinary ones. Wine serves to remind you to savor the bread and the care with which it was baked. It helps you appreciate other rituals such as the Tea Ceremony, elevating life through special activity. It calls to mind that, in addition to the jolt of caffeine awakening you to a new day, you are enjoying a specially chosen taste of coffee.*

Indeed, FoodSpirit or LifeSpirit—the joys of nature, of art, and of all manner of marvels in daily life—provide ongoing invitations to see and celebrate the countless blessings of life. Wine, however, represents a unique spiritual access point that exists, in its essence, to shed light on all the others that await your notice and acknowledgment.

REFLECTION QUESTIONS FOR SIPPIN':

1. What special treats or tastes in your day awaken you to the preciousness of life?

2. How do music and art and _____ serve as spiritual access points?

3. How could pausing to notice and celebrate some facet of life add to the quality of the rest of your day?

4.

Finding Spirituality in the Details of the Day

Sip 59: What Does Ritual Mean to You?

You may be among those who have mixed feelings about ritual. Its positive benefits are often overshadowed by its association with boredom, or with doing something by rote; it could trigger memories of things you were forced to do that were lacking in personal meaning, without heart or soul, and that stifled spontaneity while instilling feelings of guilt for not being more respectful or responsive.

Paradoxically, the purpose of ritual is to elevate what is ordinary to the realm of what is truly special. It is not intended to be confined to religious and sacred domains. Rather, it dwells in the realm of endless possibilities for savoring the specialness of *this* moment, as it occurs. It is a mechanism and a means for stopping to notice and appreciate whatever is good and positive that may have resulted. Without the ritual of *stopping*, even momentarily—at a stop sign, as the computer reboots, during dinner, or, whenever—you risk losing nuggets of life as they slip away, unnoticed and unappreciated, forever.

Rituals associated with wine, the ways you open a bottle, let it breathe, pour the first glass to admire, to swirl, to taste, and so on, serve to remind you to see the intricacy of details that accompany otherwise brief moments. Each mini detail has its own lesson, its own meaning. All you have to do is stop, observe, and reflect on what is going on.

The more you learn, or re-learn, about the purpose and meaning of rituals, whether over a glass of wine or in a formal religious setting, the more you may choose to reconnect with observances that could awaken you to abundant opportunities each day to pause and see specialness in a moment and in the blessing of being alive.

One way to increase such consciousness is to see it in the moment you clink glasses, share best wishes, and sit and enjoy another taste of the many fruits of this amazing world.

REFLECTION QUESTIONS FOR SIPPIN':

1. What part of your day contains a ritual that is lost in the mindless rote of seemingly endless repetition?

2. What would be the difference if you were mindful of an otherwise repetitive moment?

3. What ritual could you think of as a positive example that you could apply in bringing more ceremony into other facets of your life?

4.

Sip 60: When Does Pouring Wine Celebrate the Golden Rule?

Knowing something about a wine, where the grapes were grown or who crafted it, could add measures of appreciation for the care with which it was made.

Many winemakers are passionate about their work, turning a carefully tended vine into a delicious-tasting wine. They rejoice in anticipation of people enjoying the results of their efforts.

There is something wonderful about pausing to appreciate the love and care that went into a particular wine, and it is particularly special when one can speak from personal knowledge about a wine and/or its winemaker.

Reflecting on what the winemaker has given for consumers to enjoy invites those about to do so to channel that energy and give something to each other: Taking turns and pouring the wine for one another could be a special tasting of the Golden Rule.

Considering steps of cooperation and mutual support that go into transforming grapes to wine, pouring for one another, is a connecting ritual, awakening you to endless possibilities for applying the Golden Rule as an ongoing strategy for strengthening relationships and engaging special times.

It could remind you to seek opportunities to hear and benefit from each other's stories and wisdom, sharing tastes of life.

REFLECTION QUESTIONS FOR SIPPIN':

1. How does pouring for another, serving someone else, serve your needs?

2. What rituals could you think of that helped you connect with someone and something special in your past?

3.

Sip 61: What is Wonderful about Clinking Glasses?

What makes wine inherently spiritual is that, in opening it and pouring a glass, you create an opportunity for a toast to celebrate the moment.

What you do, or do not do, with that opportunity could impact the rest of the evening. It is easy to go on autopilot in ritualistic and repetitive situations, like shaking hands and asking, "How are you?"

Clinking glasses could be a typical repetitive moment that slips by, or an instant of awareness of something and someone special.

What is in a clink? What is in a handshake? It might well be what you feel in giving a hug: caring and sharing and reminding yourself how important that is. Such moments make the evening special.

Wine and spirituality connect when we connect.

A good wish is always in the air: "Have a nice day," "Make it a good one." The key is to put yourself into the words, and to turn them into deeds. Doing so, clinking an elevated glass of wine, is a wonderful way to elevate life.

REFLECTION QUESTIONS FOR SIPPIN':

1. What instances remind you to regroup and refocus?

2. How difficult is it to give your full concentration some, most, or all of the time?

3. What does wine have to do with saying hello or good-bye?

4.

Sip 62: How Do the Mondavis Bring Spirituality Alive?

In creating a WineSpirit video conversation with the late Robert Mondavi, at age 90, (joined by wife Margrit) in 2003, it became clear that Robert's life and teaching of what he identified as the Good Life, was actually a blueprint for spirituality, as characterized in WineSpirit. Here are a few of the insights they shared:

Robert: "Brought up with wine, as part of the daily menu, I never saw my mother or father abuse it. ... Wine in moderation, for most people, is good for them. ... We need to educate the people that, except for those who are allergic, which can happen with any food, wine is good and healthy for you."

From Robert's 15 principles, elaborated in his book Harvests of Joy: "(Wine) enhances food, it reduces stress, it encourages friendships, it kindles romance, and, in moderation, it helps digestion; it protects the heart, promotes good health, and it improves our disposition; if abused, it is unsafe, potentially dangerous, and decidedly uncivilized."

Robert: "A good wine is gentle, friendly, and harmonizes with food; and that extends to people."

Margrit described her appreciation for Robert: "I never met a man as honest; he sees truth and expresses it with passion for wine and tremendous energy for life, and an openness to still see and learn and try new things. ... He is fun to be with! What is so special are the daily occasions when Robert selects the wine and I cook the meal, then sitting together. Those are our finest hours."

The truth about spirituality, so vividly portrayed through Robert's life and teaching, is that it is not easy, convenient, otherworldly, or something apart from daily life and its challenges. It isn't about everything happening just the way we hope it will, simply through faith or trust. It is awareness that to change the world for the better requires hard work and much more, as articulated in Robert's 15 principles, commitments he believed everyone, including himself, would do well to revisit at least every six months.

Robert's brief summation of our visit suggested the work to be done: "It's so simple, but we don't know how to apply it. No one has the time."

REFLECTION QUESTIONS FOR SIPPIN':

1. How does spirituality, as attributed in this context to Robert Mondavi, apply in your life?

2. Which of the above quotes from Robert and Margrit come closest to your view on spirituality?

3. How could wine in moderation, and its enhancement of food as part of daily life, add understanding to the meaning and presence of spirituality?

4.

Sip 63: Wine's Spirituality Enriches its Other Qualities

Many different areas of wine appeal to different people; it is its spiritual facet that adds value and meaning to all the others. People connect to wine as a business, agricultural product, processed food, accompaniment to cuisine, fascination, friend and muse to artists throughout time, and a healthful product—all dimensions attracting varied tastes and interests.

Wine's spiritual capacity engages all of life's complexities: work, sustenance, relationships, aesthetics, and overall health and wellness.

Some people who yearn for spirituality seek it exclusively in formal religious settings. You might not think of finding it in other parts of the day or week, however inspired you may feel as you leave the sanctuary. The problem is that this positive energy can dissipate, lost among disconnected fragments and disjointed details that fill days and weeks.

WineSpirit's goal is to bring spiritual dimensions into everyday life, in recognizing and honoring wine as a catalyst for doing so. Each part of the process that produces a glass of wine—the grape, the vineyard, and the wine itself—encourages connectivity between all of life's fragments, and invites a quest for greater balance, with satisfaction and delight in wholeness emerging from the pieces.

REFLECTION QUESTIONS FOR SIPPIN':

1. Where do you seek and find spirituality?

2. What connections could you make between wine's spiritual nature and its other properties?

3. How difficult is it for you to associate spirituality with aspects of life beyond formal religious settings?

4.

Sip 64: How Could You Make the *S* Word (Spirituality) More User-Friendly?

In conversation with Brother Timothy, who was winemaker for The Christian Brothers during Prohibition, he mused that had society understood wine not as an instrument of intoxication, but rather as a contributing force for fellowship, relationship, and religious or spiritual expression, it could have qualified for exemption from the laws addressing drunkenness. The problem: a superficial reality had uprooted a deeper one.

Along with loss of awareness of wine's spiritual moorings, is a parallel loss of awareness of spirituality's function and place in ongoing daily life. For many people, spirituality resides in confined places: formal religious sanctuaries.

While you can access spirituality through wine in certain religious settings, you could also easily do so through toasts at your dinner table. Wine encourages you to experience reality more as balance and integration, and less as compartmentalization and fragmentation.

You could think of the "*S*" word as "special" rather than "spiritual," and increasingly seek and find interactions in your day that are special, and worth noticing and cherishing. In stringing together a number of them, you could discover that seemingly disjointed fragments now connect as part of a larger whole.

From ancient times, wine has served as a reminder: This moment is not just another disjointed fragment. What could you do to see how special this moment really is?

In looking within and more closely at those with whom you are sharing an experience, you could find yourself moving along a path of increasing specialness, and in so doing, infuse the "S" word more frequently into your life.

REFLECTION QUESTIONS FOR SIPPIN':

1. How is your definition of spirituality shaped by your religious upbringing?

2. What obstacles do you face in thinking of a conversation about wine's meaning in your life as being a spiritual experience?

3. What happens to your perspective when you go through a period of unusually special interactions?

4.

Sip 65: How Do Moments in the Past Enrich Today's Presence?

In a Jewish sanctification of the Sabbath eve, a celebrant holds a cup of wine or grape juice and recalls, in chanting a blessing called Kiddush, two moments from the past that infuse the present one with heightened significance.

The first originates in the biblical story of Creation, the envisioning of structure, order, and goodness for life in this physical realm. The crowning moment, predating human consciousness, is the creation of the seventh day, the Sabbath, the gift of *stopping* to rest and take stock, introduced along with life itself as part of the genetics of life.

In the story of the creation of the Sabbath, a life-transforming word is introduced: "Kadosh" ("Holy"), meaning that which is unique, special, set apart, memorable, treasurable, elevated, precious, transcendent, significant, outstanding, excellent, and sacred. The Creator's directive is, "Stop! And in doing so, access and enjoy life's blessings. Stop and notice. Cherish what you have heard, seen, and done."

The second point of reference celebrates Israel going out of "Egypt," (translated from Hebrew as "narrow confinement" or "constriction.") The joy of escaping slavery fuels an urge to fill life with freedom: doing good, caring, and building wonderful relationships with those likewise committed.

This ritual, with glass of wine in hand and spirit of joy in heart, blends prehistory, the genetics of life, with history, human realities. It celebrates gifts you were born with, as well as those gifts and lessons acquired along the way.

Raising your glass in this ceremony integrates what has come before with what is precious now, a blend of past and present, overflowing with blessing and significance, accessed through stopping to notice and appreciate. It welcomes you to

Day Seven, a time to re-energize, for the six upcoming days of your own creation before your next chance to *stop*.

REFLECTION QUESTIONS FOR SIPPIN':

1. How do you benefit from *stopping*?

2. What conditions and constrictions keep you from *stopping*, and what price do you pay?

3. What enslavement have you overcome, and how did doing so affect you?

4.

Sip 66: What Do You Do When a Gift Turns Bad?

Some years ago, when dear neighbors celebrated their 45th wedding anniversary, I gave them two old wines that I had been saving: a Cabernet and a Zinfandel.

A few days later Karl popped over to ask me to taste a few different wines "to get another opinion." Each wine was sour and undrinkable. He valued my input because he had just finished a cycle of medicine that had not permitted him any wine until then. He couldn't believe that three different wines would each be bad. He assumed it was the aftereffects of the medication, until I assured him it was the wine.

Then he showed me the bottles. One was the Zinfandel that I had just given him. I was both mortified and delighted. I felt awful to have given him a bad wine for his anniversary — and wonderful that he had shared what had happened. We had a good laugh, and then I brought over an even older bottle of Zinfandel; the delicious taste reassured him that the problem was not with the medicine.

Sometimes a gift of wine can be an act that opens a relationship, with a first visit. Or, as in this case, it can reflect the value in a longstanding friendship, when you can be truthful with one another.

If Karl hadn't shared the truth about the Zinfandel, he would have missed an opportunity to experience the depth and openness of our friendship. It would have also left me to assume that I had given something wonderful to dear friends, when, in fact, I hadn't.

<u>REFLECTION QUESTIONS FOR SIPPIN':</u>

1. Can you recall having a good laugh with someone about a gift or plan that went awry?

2. Is it easier to open up with a friend when you are relaxing with a glass of wine?

3. Have you ever not shared something with someone, to avoid hurt feelings, and how did you feel?

4.

(In memory of Karl and Anne Zipf)

Sip 67: How could the Ritual of Passing the Cup Apply Today?

By Paul Wagner

Last year, I gave a lecture at a major wine conference on the history of wine. One of the topics I discussed was the power of the wine cup in ancient times. In the ancient world there was usually only a single wine cup for the dinner; the cup would be passed from guest to guest as they became thirsty. The cup became a bit like a microphone—he who had the cup also had the attention of the rest of the diners, and frequently took advantage of the opportunity to make a toast, offer a blessing, or say something of particular importance.

This year, at the same conference, a woman came up to me after my lecture and reminded me of that point. As I thanked her for being so attentive, she interrupted me to tell a story.

Her husband had died just a few months ago. And she remembered my speech and how it had affected them both. As a memorial service for her husband, she invited all of the mourners to join her in one of his favorite vineyards. When they arrived there, she explained the story of the wine cup ... and passed it from guest to guest. Each was asked to take that opportunity to share some of the wine, and to share a story about her husband. She said it was a very moving event, and her daughter then joined her to tell me how much they appreciated it.

As they thanked me, I could not begin to tell them how much I appreciated their story.

REFLECTION QUESTIONS FOR SIPPIN':

1. **How does sharing, whether a thought or a sip, bring us closer to each other?**

2. How do stories cycle, from one person to another, each time gaining new meaning?

3.

Sip 68: How Has Changing Your Place Changed Your Fortune?

Many people have migrated from other places and careers to settle into life as grape growers and wine makers in vineyards you can find in almost every state in the U.S. Some recall their move to Napa as magical; changing their place led to changes of fortune, both material and spiritual.

It isn't any one thing, like grapes and vineyards, that makes being in the wine country special. It is a confluence of life conditions, beginning with partnership between humans and nature.

Change of place could also mean change of awareness and of focus. Some people can recall their first bottle of wine. They can still taste it and everything about the "place" they were in and the adventure they had shared.

The focus in toasting with wine is on elevating a moment, making it magical and occasionally so special as to take root as a lifetime memory. Such moments are in themselves changes in place, often manifested as changes in life energy, momentum, and luck.

For many people who changed their momentum and luck after changing careers and moving to wine country, it was something akin to the pull of the mountain in the movie *Close Encounters of the Third Kind.* They were drawn to this place, and this perspective on life, and they have never gone back.

REFLECTION QUESTIONS FOR SIPPIN':

1. What life changes have you made, and what were the results?

2. What is your explanation for why people have left

careers and lifestyles to live and work in the wine country?

3.

Sip 69: What Could Move an Agnostic toward the Divine?

One of the benefits of exploring relationships between wine and spirituality is an enhanced perspective on the Cosmos and its possible place in your life. This came to light in a WineSpirit seminar on wine and mysticism led by Jan Shrem of Clos Pegase winery.

The evening abounded in irony. First, Jan, an avowed agnostic, led the group in a direction WineSpirit tends not to go: questioning participants on their religious backgrounds and roots ... what such identity meant, and whether it connected in any way to wine or spirituality. In his own disclosure Jan indicated that although he was raised in a very observant Jewish home, his father engendered in him everything negative about religion and God; he never trusted that his son honored the tradition with prayer at the proper times. Even when he had done the prayer, his father accused him of lying and he had to do it again. It became easier to lie that he hadn't done it and then do it again, to avoid his father's wrath.

Raised in such a dysfunctional religious environment, he prayed that he would find a way out of his miserable life as soon as possible.

He left home at age 16 and began a life of adventure far removed from his religious roots. Eventually his journey led him to Japan, and to the woman who would become his loving wife, Mitsuko. She was the one who opened him to his passion for wine and the arts. Their partnership eventually led to constructing Clos Pegase, a magnificent winery celebrating wine, the arts, and the patron god of wine, Bacchus.

The greatest irony of the evening came to light as one of the participants suggested that God had answered Jan's prayer to get away from his father's religious persecution and his oppressive god. He was given a Godly blessing: the journey that led him away from home along a path that would enable his unique sense of spirituality to take root and flourish. That salient observation helped Jan understand, for the first time after so many years, that instead of fleeing God and escaping forever, it was God who rescued him from his misery at home and was with him, over the years, in his life of celebration of the presence of the Cosmos in all the work he loved so dearly.

Jan's "Aha!" came in finally understanding God's role in rescuing him from his miserable youth; it suggested connections, after all: with the God of wine and art and beauty, a God with which he was very much at home, and the God of his ancestors that had saved him by leading him away from home.

REFLECTION QUESTIONS FOR SIPPIN':

1. What connection, if any, can you find between religion and your feeling of wine's relationship to spirituality?

2. What "Aha!" could you recall that changed your perspective on life and values you took for granted?

3. How has your journey been influenced positively or negatively by the way you were raised?

4.

(In Appreciation of Jan Shrem)

Sip 70: When is it a Sin to Be Holy?

The Nazirite, described in the biblical book Numbers, chapter 6:1-21, made a vow of abstinence for a limited period of time in order to engage a process of spiritual purification. The teaching in this chapter was that one who vowed not to drink wine (among several abstentions) elevated himself to a level of holiness akin to the High Priest of biblical times. Yet this very Nazirite had to bring a sin offering at the termination of his vow. The Talmud, Jewish rabbinic law of nearly 2,000 years ago, explained: This sacrificial offering was to atone for the sin of denying himself the pleasure of wine. Thus, the vow that elevated him to holiness had caused him to sin. Why?

According to the Talmudic interpretation, God created the world for humans to enjoy in their service to the Creator. The idea was to enjoy the permitted fruits of this world, not to refrain from them. Just as the universe was an extension of the Creator's domain, so people were to engage the physical world, in moderation, and in so doing, to connect to that power. They were to elevate and sanctify the physical realm but not allow themselves to become addicted to materialism, devoid of spirituality. In entering the World-to-Come, the afterlife, people would have to account for everything in this world they were permitted to enjoy, yet did not.

Wine in moderation, though forbidden to the Nazirite, could serve to enhance human behavior and accentuate occasions of joy, helping give a voice to innermost sentiments. When abused, consumed without moderation, it degrades people, robbing them of their most precious possession, the mind.

Recognizing a weakness, and choosing abstinence over abuse, could render one holy. But lest the Nazirite lose sight of the ideal, the teaching emphasized that he was nevertheless a sinner. He had lost touch with one of life's goals: enjoying with gratitude what you are permitted of this world. Were he on the ideal plane, he would not have to abstain from wine; he would utilize it as part of spiritual life. Thus, the vow that rendered him holy compromised a life-affirming ideal.

The Torah implies that the purpose of choosing the vow of the Nazirite was not abstinence for its own sake, but as a lesson for properly drinking wine afterward, and in so doing, becoming sanctified and uplifted.

REFLECTION QUESTIONS FOR SIPPIN':

1. What is your experience of fasting or other ritual vows as a way to elevate consciousness and/or access other levels of spirituality or purification?

2. How do you understand the teaching that this world is here for you to enjoy, without it necessarily resulting in too much self-indulgence?

3. What facets of ritual or religious behavior do you find helpful in heightening your appreciation of life?

4.

(With thanks to Rabbi Zev Leff and his biblical commentary on the Nazirite)

Sip 71: How Do Wine Growers Treat the Land?

Some Napa old-timers wonder whether newer arrivals adequately appreciate the sanctity and preciousness of the agricultural zone, where grapes are grown and wine produced. How mindful are custodians of vineyards and wine-producing facilities of the importance of taking good care of the land?

One fear is that the growth of corporate-run wineries could diminish the character unique to family owned operations, and that larger and newer conglomerates will lose sight of the custodial nature of their work. Theirs is a sacred responsibility, to protect the land they till and be mindful of seeking good relations with neighbors and surrounding communities.

One interpretation of the biblical story of Creation is that human life emerged on Day Six to teach partnership with the Divine in responsibility and care for the land. The first mention of working the land was of Noah planting a vineyard.

City dwellers identify property as *real* estate yet, ironically, in cities the land's concretization has made it less real; whatever natural land remains is designated as parks or open space.

Part of Napa's specialness, as is the case in other wine growing regions, is its agricultural nature. Prioritizing preservation of the land and soil produces wonderful yields of all manner of blessing; much of that harvest is wine. The Ag zone is home to the *real* estate. It is good when those who tend this land and live their lives on its soil are vigilant in protecting the gift and keeping its trust faithfully and fruitfully.

REFLECTION QUESTIONS FOR SIPPIN':

1. How is the partnership of human and nature magical?

2. How do where you live and your livelihood influence, negatively or positively, your awareness of the balance between human and nature?

3.

Sip 72: How Molecules of Water
and Wine Added Meaning to Life

Sondra Barrett, Ph.D., a scientist, chemist, photographer, teacher, (and author of Sips 7 and 84), shared this insight at a WineSpirit retreat: *"Looking 'within,' through a microscope, at forms made by wine molecules, one sees things that are surprising and awe-inspiring, especially in observing wine at different ages. The molecules are 'simple' in the young wine, more complex in aging, and at full maturation, emanate 'light.' The light begins to show itself only with the growth of spirit in the brew, during fermentation. As the wine declines with age, the light grows dim. The life cycle of these molecular forms suggests truths too subtle to see without the aid of the scope. Do people not grow in just that way?"*

Sondra shared wine's innermost essence and the lessons, therein, as part of a day when spirituality flowed. It was a day filled with engaging different perspectives and points of view, springing from these questions: *What matters to you? Why are you here ... in the wine country ... exploring wine and its place in your life?*

Two and a half hours later than planned, the group stepped outside, for continued reflection in the Sauvignon Blanc vineyard. From there, they ambled down the slope to the Napa River, where everyone beheld something amazing: the river was running its normal course, at its usual pace, except *backward*, heading determinedly upstream toward its origins. Molecules of Nature bursting forth this day had created something extraordinary.

Overlooking the river, the group sat for a while in quiet reflection; it was special, if brief. In the few minutes of shared thoughts and feelings, the river became still, preparing to resume its predictable path to the sea. While the influence of high tide on a tidal river explained the how, nothing could explain the timing. Being two hours late so as to unknowingly be on time for a natural event, was one of many molecules of life that flowed that day. It was a *super natural* topping to a day in which 12 people actually found what they were seeking.

The takeaway, simple and pervasive: Spirituality is natural, ongoing, and vitalizing energy, in and of life, whose molecules comprise everyday living. Living in that energy is what life is all about.

REFLECTION QUESTIONS FOR SIPPIN':

1. **What encounters with nature do you recall that expanded your definition of spirituality?**

2. **How does heightened awareness of something special going on influence your attitude and perspective beyond that experience?**

3. **How does grounding something spiritual in scientific terms, as in molecules of wine mirroring your experience of wine, broaden your view of the magic and mystery of life?**

4.

(With thanks to Sondra Barrett)

Harvesting Wisdom of the Ages

For 10,000 years, man has connected wine with the spiritual—the drink of the gods, the blood of God. And each period throughout history has added to this tapestry.

Each generation adds a new chapter, but the story continues, unchanged.

Sip 73: How Do You Recharge Spiritual Batteries?

One drawback to battery-powered appliances is that they can suddenly run out of juice. With re-chargeable batteries, you can at least maintain their charge and minimize surprises as well as waste. Otherwise, barring blackouts, electricity keeps everything going—especially people. Who has time to sleep, with lights always on somewhere and business meetings a mouse-click or video conference away?

What about human power? People are not electrically generated as much as *battery powered*. Nor is it a disposable battery. Human batteries need recharging the old-fashioned way, in a charger known by many names: *sleep, rest, meditation, heart-to-heart, retreat, vacation, coffee break, weekend, afternoon tea, relaxing meal*—all moments that re-energize.

Recharging human batteries involves more than regaining physical strength and stamina with a few hours of sleep. Just as important is charging and re-charging spiritual batteries, making time to breathe in special moments, renew relationships, regain perspective, and remember that life is full of details worth noticing and savoring.

Since antiquity, people have honored and consecrated moments of renewal through the enjoyment of wine. As religious connector in church, or catalyst for sanctifying time in synagogue, or to celebrate special times with family and friends over heartfelt toasts, wine elevates the moment. The ritual of raising a glass of wine indicates something special is under way.

Such moments recharge spiritual batteries. They re-energize people, leaving them ready to go—and ready to stop again from time to time, to breathe in miracles of life. The key is to remember the importance of stopping *to renew and refocus, in bringing more great moments to life.*

<u>REFLECTION QUESTIONS FOR SIPPIN':</u>

1. What are best ways to keep your "batteries" charged?

2. What happens when they get depleted?

3. Where and how does spirituality fit in your life?

4.

Sip 74: How Could Vines and Veins Awaken You to Life?

Many images associated with wine suggest taking a long view of life and a multi-generational grasp of its significance.

Vines carry the flow of life wherever and however they grow. They also carry memory of life that was. The vine and its fruit go back 10,000 years, predating human memory. A vine brings into being the one fruit that has been the taste of life's most precious, most important, and oftentimes, happiest moments, elevated to consciousness through the magic of toasts and well-wishing.

Wine's long and storied history extends to antiquity.

It is a tale of "vines" and "veins," identical letters, intertwining. Veins carry life's flow, pumped through the heart, enabling you to be well, give thanks, and to toast with the fruit of the vine. Veins and vines, heart and soul, intersect in a moment's toast; fruit of the vine turns life, flowing through the veins, into consciousness of blessing.

What a wondrous and strategic partnership. From earliest antiquity, the fruit of the vine, consecrated to Life, has brought consciousness of blessing to light. Deriving strength and inspiration in wine's ceremonial application, people from the outset have persevered in their long, tortuous, and enduring trails of discovery: that life is a miracle worthy of notice and praise, with new meaning and new insight always awaiting revelation and celebration.

The long and tangled threads of veins and vines bring you to this moment, to raise glasses and exult, with thanks, for those you are with and for whatever it is that keeps you alive and allows you to be here, another taste of the miracle of life.

REFLECTION QUESTIONS FOR SIPPIN':

1. How far have we come in 10,000 years?

2. What ancestral memories of celebrating with wine are pieces of your family history?

3. How do your internal feelings intertwine with external factors to provide perspective on how life is meaningful to you?

4.

Sip 75: What is Your Prescription for Health?

One of wine's characteristics is its potential for intoxication. One of life's characteristics is its propensity for stress.

Times for clinking glasses and sharing good wishes are moments set apart from pressures, deadlines, and constant struggles to keep up. A glass of wine at the end of a day is a way to savor the best of today, and to be "up" for tomorrow.

There are many drugs and pharmaceuticals used to address life's ailments and pains. Wine is a "prescription" for calm in precarious times, and it includes the same caution found on every drug and pharmaceutical label: "Take the prescribed quantity, and no more."

Wine's health benefits are predicated on consumption in moderation: physical health, with red wine good for the heart, and white wine, according to one study, good for the lungs; and spiritual health, manifesting in the relaxing character of a glass of wine, subtly enhancing the taste of the food, and the enjoyment of those sharing the experience. *As a drug for life, wine invites you to bring the best into and out of yourself in special times, with special people. The instructions on the label add, "Find more of life's moments to celebrate as an antidote to overload, anxiety, and stress."*

In difficult times, it is good to have friends and colleagues with whom to share support and care. Through good times and bad, each toast induces you to reflect on your relationships, strengthen them, and savor them. Pausing to do so is good medicine for keeping up with everything life sends your way.

REFLECTION QUESTIONS FOR SIPPIN':

1. How is wine good medicine in your life?

2. What remedies help you respond to life's pressures

and enable you to see and feel what is good and blessed about your lot?

3. What strategies do you utilize to make time to stop, breathe, and regain your balance?

4.

Sip 76: How Do You Age Gracefully?

Wines and people are a lot alike. Both are shaped by their earliest years and the growing conditions that set their journeys into motion.

Wines develop in character through the ways they are blended and the conditions in which they are kept, with the goal of achieving balance. Some do better than others.

We are all products of growing conditions, and the influences of the relationships we have developed. Some of us are more fortunate than others in the achievement of life balance, in our marriages and through important friendships and associations.

Like wine, we age — and hopefully, do it gracefully.

In the cold of winter, when the vines that will bear new life are dormant, we find ourselves left to our thoughts and memories of warmer days and dreams of what spring and a new cycle might bring.

On New Year's Day, we can add to the traditional toast, "Out with the old and in with the new," a word of appreciation for the old, and for the maturation that comes with our growing abilities to face what is new with increasing wisdom and satisfaction.

The taste of a ripe old wine can remind you that aging isn't so bad. Celebrating being "another year older" is an opportunity to add the rest of the thought — "and wiser." Cherish the knowledge that you are older and wiser.

With each sip of wine and every passing day, may you find increasing satisfaction in who you are, who you have become, and the people and events that have contributed to your life's journey. Cheers!

REFLECTION QUESTIONS FOR SIPPIN':

1. What are your attitudes about aging?

2. What characteristics have you seen in people who have aged well?

3. What wines have you particularly enjoyed because they changed for the better with age?

4.

Sip 77: What Are You Planting for the Future?

The late Al Brounstein, founder of Diamond Creek Vineyard, made a striking comment in a WineSpirit video conversation: His wines would outlive him, he said, because they would be drinking well for a hundred years. However accurate his prediction will be, the insight is sobering. A winemaker can produce something that could possibly outlive her or him.

These precarious times invite reflection. Where are you in the cycle of life? What have you planted? What have you harvested? What have you tasted and savored of life's sweetness along your way?

It doesn't matter what work you do; a part of you will remain after you are gone. You weave a life story each day; you sow seeds and nurture relationships in unique ways; you never know the full impact that you have on others.

Unlike a well-built cabinet that may last a century or more, wine will meet a sudden end in serving the purpose for which it was crafted: a celebration of life, a blessing of abundance, a prayer for peace, a wish for good health, a thank you for special memories, a toast for the future.

In a time of acute awareness that tomorrow is not a certainty, you could appreciate this moment more than ever before and add it to those already in your treasure chest of memories.

You might not reap all the harvests you plant, but you could feel blessed in knowing that what you do plant will benefit and provide something of value to those coming after you.

That is what helped Al Brounstein endure well over 20 years of Parkinson's disease, until his death, in 2006. He enjoyed knowing that he had turned a beautiful piece of land called Diamond Creek into even greater beauty, with eye-catching waterfalls, colorful gardens, and precious grape harvests that will perpetuate the work of a particular man years after he planted his vineyards and labored with such love along that way.

REFLECTION QUESTIONS FOR SIPPIN':

1. How could reflection on what you will leave behind influence what you are doing now?

2. What tangible gifts do you possess from someone no longer alive?

3. How does coming to grips with the uncertainty of tomorrow impact the quality of your life today?

4.

Sip 78: What is the Risk in Saving Wine for Another Day?

A Sip written shortly after September 11, 2001, was based on an observation made in response to that horrifying event: *"It no longer made sense to hold onto so many older wines for some future special occasion. Who could know what might happen tomorrow, that we will even make it to that day?"*

This sobering insight came to mind again in the midst of the unimaginable horror of the December 2004 tsunami in Asia. So many communities wiped off the map ... impossible to comprehend. Many of the dead were tourists, having the times of their lives—for the last time. Little does any of us know what tomorrow might bring, given the unrelenting threat of terrorism, and its randomness, in addition to the rest of life's unknowns.

Many people pour their life into their work, to assure good things for their family's future. This is right and good to do, though it has serious risks and consequences. Too many forget to treasure *today* in all its conditions, even the stress and the struggle. More people align with TGIF than get excited about Monday. Vacation is held in higher regard than the crush of an overscheduled workday. The sun will come out tomorrow ...

Yet, it is more important to keep in mind that just being alive, and having people in your life and programs in which you are involved, is the stuff of life worth cherishing. Living responsibly, in helping others grow, is worth appreciating each step along the way. You can continue to plan for the future, but *this* is what you have now and it is worth celebrating or commemorating. You are creating memories for tomorrow.

It would be good to look in the cellar and ask yourself which bottles are being saved for a particular occasion, and which could serve to render this evening a memory worth making. It behooves you to do the same with all of your possessions.

What resources are you saving that you could put toward relief efforts and helping others during the economic tsunami of 2009, without diminishing your own security too much?

As hard as it was to raise glasses and welcome 2005 after hearing of the Asian tsunami, and to do so for 2009 in the midst of the economic devastation, you could always toast to hope and to love, and pledge to give what you have today, that others might make it to tomorrow, trusting that somehow you will make it as well, and with each other's help, make tomorrow better.

REFLECTION QUESTIONS FOR SIPPIN':

1. Does knowing someone personally affected make it more likely for you to give?

2. How much stuff do you hold onto for some future use?

3. What analogy comes to mind as to how you feel when you share or part with a wine you love?

4.

Sip 79: Life ... What Are You Saving It For?

One of life's great unknowns is how long any of us will live. Tragic accidents and catastrophic events bring that reality into focus. Not knowing how long you have is good cause to approach daily activity with greater focus and appreciation, Events, experiences, and memories are often overlooked or forgotten in the assumption that there is so much more to look forward to tomorrow and for years to come.

Al Brounstein and Jamie Davies, neighbors in Calistoga, California, created some of Napa Valley's finest wines: one, prestigious Cabernets from four distinct vineyards, the other, world-class sparkling wines. Al labored in the vineyard for over 20 years under the shadow of a killer, Parkinson's disease. In building Diamond Creek, he was motivated and even energized by this disease to dedicate every day to making a treasured wine in a place of awe and beauty, an environment he created and shaped. He did so by planting magnificent rose gardens and building inspiring waterfalls, enhancing the terroir throughout the estate. He responded to Parkinson's by giving his best each day. Al accomplished much, all but vanquishing the disease for many more years than anyone could have imagined, though it ultimately took him in summer 2006.

Al's neighbor, Jamie Davies of Schramsberg, had a briefer battle with Parkinson's. Yet, like him, in the years she lived with it until her passing in early 2008, she never stopped engaging each day to its fullest, continuing with her activities, such as participating on the Napa Community Foundation in a period that saw tremendous growth. Jamie's only concession to the disease was slowing down physically as she moved between activities. Like Al, in all her years she took nothing for granted, especially not her stewardship of the historic Schram estate, made famous in its early days by Robert Louis Stevenson.

Jamie and her husband Jack understood they were custodians, here to tend the land and preserve it so others might enjoy it after they were gone.

Sitting with Al in his final hours, I experienced a man who had overcome all obstacles to accomplish so much and who now faced the unknown frontier with wisdom, grace, and his trademark wit. He promised he would never stop searching for the one who took his hand and said, "Shake!" (one of Parkinson's symptoms), so that the spell might finally be lifted.

Al's wife Boots carries on with Al's mission in this world, not only with the work of the vineyard, but also in continuing to search for that wizard. Boots hosts an annual gala event, raising vital funds to continue the fight to cure Parkinson's.

REFLECTION QUESTIONS FOR SIPPIN':

1. **To what degree does assuming you have unlimited time allow you to overlook some of today?**

2. **When you focus more closely on details, and choices you face today, what difference does that make?**

3. **How does losing someone dear affect you in areas beyond the loss itself?**

4.

Sip 80: How Does Happenstance Contribute to Who or Where You Are Today?

Tim Hanni is one of only a few Masters of Wine in the United States, but the first time he took the exam to qualify for that degree, he failed miserably. In fact, the instructor struggled to find suitable words to discourage any thought of a re-test. All he could say was "Stay away for a very long time. Don't try this again!"

Rather than heed that advice, Tim went to work figuring out what went wrong. He realized that, with a major part of the test being in essay form, he needed to address the cause of his failure. It wasn't lack of knowledge—he knew the material well. What he lacked were organizational skills, the particular ability to use outlines and present clear thoughts. Tim enrolled in a three-day intensive seminar called "Clear Writing and Communication." He arrived at 8 a.m, on the first day and saw a sign that said, "Welcome to the Technical Skills Communication Seminar!" Tim quickly realized he had somehow enrolled in a seminar on technical writing for electronic engineers. What happened to the seminar he had planned to take? It had taken place the previous week.

Tim was understated in describing what he did next. He stayed with that seminar, though clueless about almost everything going on. In doing so, he discovered a teaching that would change his life. The electronic engineers were being taught how to communicate their technical systems for products and development, in sales, in marketing, and in helping consumers learn to use the product.

Two things happened: First, Tim discovered how to organize thoughts in a way that worked well for him. Second, and even more important, was a teaching that demanded clear definitions of every word and thought, rigor around every word and every concept used. The seminar looked at anything that in any way might be misconstrued or unclear. The teaching was simple: "Define, define, and define!"

If he had not stuck with that seminar, Tim would not have passed the Master of Wine exam, and he wouldn't be doing any of what he is doing today. Words that took on new meaning with wine include flavor, taste, aroma, and bouquet. Tim is passionate about helping people to learn to define these words for themselves, and to apply the discipline of such definition broadly in life, contributing to clearer communication and better understanding. Tim's life experience indicates that doing so changes everything: life meaning, purpose, and the power of passion in making *this* moment great.

REFLECTION QUESTIONS FOR SIPPIN':

1. In your life, how has a desired outcome resulted from unlikely events?

2. What experience that came out of adapting to the unexpected contributed to who and where you are today?

3. Which chance experiences or encounters had an impact on your orientation, today, to wine or spirituality?

4.

(With thanks to Tim Hanni)

Sip 81: How Does Wine Celebrate Community and Rebirth Through the Ages?

By Paul Wagner

I teach a class at Napa Valley College called "A Cultural Appreciation of Wine" in which we discuss the role of wine in society and culture throughout the ages, from prehistory to the present day. It is a remarkable experience, as much for the contributions that students bring to class—food, wine, and stimulating conversation—as for anything I can offer. We study everything from Ancient Sumer, the Greek Symposium, and the Roman orgies, to Victorian dinner parties and the role of wine today. Throughout all of these experiences, there is a thread, common to all cultures, when it comes to wine.

In teaching the history of wine, I begin by asking students to imagine a time long before history. Winemaking is a communal project almost by definition. You need many people to pick the grapes, crush them, and work together to press the juice from the skins. From the time of our earliest ancestors, wine must have been a glorious group celebration of the riches of the harvest—a symbol that life is good, and the gods love us.

Wine has always been more celebratory, more seasonal, than beer. Grain will last a long time, if stored properly, but wine has a definite moment of harvest, a time of fermentation. That moment coincides with the riches of the harvest of other crops as well. With limited storage conditions, early wine would oxidize and spoil rather quickly. But, it also would have been consumed long before it went bad. So wine was not only a rare pleasure, it was a symbol of the season of plenty—a way to celebrate, to prolong that season, and a way to get intoxicated. Imagine the celebrations.

And, in its own way, the grapevine has always been a

symbol of rebirth. In a single magical season, the grapevine transforms itself from a seemingly dead stick to the producer of the greatest fruit known to man. It is no wonder that early Christians often pictured a risen Christ wreathed in grapevines or standing in a tub of grapes.

In almost every early culture, wine was revered as the blood of God (The Italian grape Sangiovese literally translates as "blood of Jove") or the drink of the gods. It is a way to bring people together and create both communion and community. Even today, in our more industrial society, the grape harvest is an obvious season of celebration—both social and religious.

REFLECTION QUESTIONS FOR SIPPIN':

1. How much of the day are you alone, and how much in relationship, and what are the advantages of each?

2. What do you suppose you learn from a history of wine that you won't learn in other history courses?

3. What lessons from the past would you recommend applying today?

4.

Sip 82: How Could You Turn a Bad Wine into a Very Good One?

A home winemaker and his partner were so eager to make wine that, when they found a source for Zinfandel grapes in Paso Robles, they jumped at the chance. Here is their story:

"The grapes were deliciously ripe, and my partner's winery lab technicians recommended a very hearty yeast. Home winemakers are usually worried about getting fruit that's ripe enough, or a 'stuck' fermentation. Therefore, we weren't 'watching our flank', you might say, and the sweetness of the fruit together with the hearty yeast produced a wine with 17.5 percent alcohol. It was undrinkable. So, we wracked our brains and in the moment of giving up, when my mind let go of conscious control, my inner wisdom (which is always at work, anyway) pushed its way into my consciousness. I said, at that moment, 'Of course! It has to be Port!'" And a delicious Port it was, as all who tasted it attested."

It is one thing for a winemaker to work with a particular varietal and take necessary measures to add flavor, balance, and character to a wine. It is another matter to take a failed wine and *reposition* it, as an entirely different kind of wine, not suitable for consumption with a main course, but instead as a delightful after-dinner drink. It is poetic that what emerged instead of Zinfandel was Port, a wine associated with the smooth and satisfying close to a lovely evening, a taste suggesting all is well with life.

That particular Port was its own reward, an unexpected blessing. Its existence suggested that, no matter how badly things seem to go, when you allow for other possibilities and different approaches, you may yet reach that point in the evening, where, glass of Port in hand, you look back and see so much that went well that day.

Clearly, the resources you could make good use of include inner imagination, intuition, and letting go of the need to have things go the way you intended. One home winemaker let go of tight controls, of a belief in the way things had to be, and accessed inner awareness and creative forces that allowed for a wonderful and different outcome.

It seems that lemons have no monopoly on becoming lemonade.

REFLECTION QUESTIONS FOR SIPPIN':

1. How have you, or someone you know, turned lemons into lemonade, or too much of a good thing into something better?

2. What resources do you have, that you overlook or underappreciate, when life doesn't "work" or go as intended?

3. What attributes are conducive to creating lemonade, to turning bad into good?

4.

(With thanks to Doug Ramo)

Sip 83: How Does Culture Grow from the Ground Up?

It is amazing what you can see in the English language when you look closely and reflect. WineSpirit Chairman David Freed was in conversation with food and wine aficionado Mark Linder during a break at the Unified Wine Symposium in Sacramento. Mark pointed out that "agriculture" reflects how people derived meaning in life. The planting, growing, and gathering of food is cyclical and rhythmic, with busy times and quiet times. In quiet times, people could and did stop to reflect on meanings of life. The word contains the process: "Agri" connected to the cycle of tending the land, and providing food for sustenance and survival; "culture" indicated a capacity to have time to reflect and make sense of life and transmit its meanings to a future generation.

There are few English words that contain the word "culture": "agriculture", "horticulture," "viticulture," "viniculture," "multi-culture," and "subculture." Agriculture pertains to the food that is grown; horticulture covers plants and vegetation that generate oxygen to breathe. Viticulture and viniculture are about growing grapes, and making wine, used to consecrate and celebrate quality of life and of time. Multi-culture and subculture address life's variety, and contexts in which we live, including wine with which to relax and reflect on life's complexity and manifold blessings.

Later that day, in Napa, as part of a discussion, a staff member from a local market and liquor store answered a WineSpirit question: How is wine different from other agricultural products? Her response: You need food to survive, but not wine; you need wine to signify and celebrate quality in life, making life worth living.

The words that contain "culture" imply two facets of human history and ongoing conditions. First is survival: to have food to eat in order to live and to appreciate what has sustained you and keeps you alive. Second, is to have enough time to enjoy life and to reflect on sources of such enjoyment. Since antiquity, that "culture" of appreciation has included wine. Through that culture, people found ways to endure hurt and suffering with trust and belief that good times would follow. Those who survived, and reached moments of celebration and accomplishment, would hold onto and treasure the memories of those good times when lean times returned, as they tend to do in cycles of life.

May your next glass of wine celebrate good health, good times, happy memories, and lots of new ones on the way!

REFLECTION QUESTIONS FOR SIPPIN':

1. How does a glass of wine help you separate from the stress of daily survival?

2. How much of your day feels like survival and how much is savoring life's blessings and qualities?

3.

(With thanks to Mark Linder)

Harvesting Wisdom of the Ages

Sip 84: Wine Sex: Do Wines Have a Gender?

By Sondra Barrett

Are there feminine or masculine wines? The grape from which beverages vinous are produced has a checkered sexual past. In the beginning of grape's rooting into this planet, it was heterosexual. One vine was female, another male. Both were needed to produce fruit. Wine was a result of a marriage between two different sexual plants.

Due to human intervention, all that is changed. The grapevine is now bisexual, a hermaphrodite. It can fertilize itself. It no longer needs another plant. But it does need us to harvest its treasures. The vine's original heterosexual nature, one plant needing another, created an endless display of genetic variants. Only when the plant became bisexual could relative stability of grape varieties be obtained. Today we have about 600 different varietals worldwide, 240 varieties in the U.S.

So, since the plant has both sexual tendencies, could a voluptuous feminine wine be made, as well as a brawny male? Once more, human intervention helps define fruitful sexual expression. In your wine drinking experience, have you discovered wines that show sexual proclivities?

Here are a few of mine: Chardonnay, when it's rich and creamy sliding into my mouth, is clearly female. I've never met a male Chardonnay, but have experienced a sleeker, leaner female version when the wine is made without malolactic fermentation. Karen MacNeil, in *The Wine Bible*, might call that the "Jamie Lee Curtis" Chardonnay, whereas the full-bodied style is "Marilyn Monroe." Aggressive bold Cabernet Sauvignon is always masculine to me, as is crisp, angular Sauvignon Blanc. Merlot is female, as are many Pinot Noirs.

A wine's microscopic signatures give more clues to its sexual orientation. In the language of symbols and sacred geometry, rounded curved forms are feminine—think the Earth, moon, circles, and the womb. Linear angular forms, like swords, squares, triangles and, dare I include the male organ, are masculine shapes. From the microscopic perspective, fluid, soft-looking forms are more predominant in *feminine* wines whereas what I call *masculine* wines express lots of sharp shapes tending towards angularity.

REFLECTION QUESTIONS FOR SIPPIN':

1. How does the grapevine's dual sexual nature remind you of how you balance our own male and female tendencies—or do you?

2. When you are feeling aggressive or docile, which wine do you prefer to drink?

3. Are certain varietals more masculine?

4. And aren't we fortunate that, early on, humans discovered how to bring the best out in their vines to expand their abilities?

5.

(Inspired by a WineSpirit Seminar led by Paul Wagner)

Sip 85: How Could Breaking Some Rules Bring the Best to Life?

One "rule" in serving wine concerns the matter of temperature, with red commonly served at room temperature, and white wine chilled. Since room temperature today tends to be warmer than people used to keep their homes, serving a red at a typically warm room temperature might contribute to it opening up and finishing more quickly than it would had it been chilled, or just left on a windowsill in the cool autumn breeze. Slightly chilling a red wine will likely bring out more of its taste and character. Chilling it slightly allows it to remain enjoyable throughout a meal. The typically observed "rule" of serving reds at room temperature is a case of following a time-honored standard that might result in a less rewarding outcome.

An analogy could be drawn in the ways that women and men stereotypically tend to treat themselves and each other. The assumption is that women are more sensitive, empathic, feeling, intuitive, and emotional than men. Men are tougher, gruffer, less sensitive, less emotional, more practical, more analytical, and more distant. They are bred to compete, stand on their own, and withstand whatever pressures come their way. Asking for directions is out of the question. They have to figure it out for themselves.

Increasingly, behaviorists are uncovering and teaching that certain "masculine" traits are found in females, and "feminine" traits in males.

While a white wine is chilled to enable it to be at its best, interestingly, many a chardonnay would benefit from less chilling. And a surprise for many is that a big, bold, and powerful red wine will benefit from chilling, albeit, to a lesser degree than the white.

If people could apply such treatment to wine, enhancing its nature and character, how much more could this increasing awareness and appreciation for complexities in men and women contribute to more meaningful and rewarding relationships.

REFLECTION QUESTIONS FOR SIPPIN':

1. What stereotypes fuel your attitude about people?

2. What are some assumptions you make about wine?

3. What factors have contributed to your revising an opinion about a person or a wine?

4.

Sip 86: What Does TGIF Mean to You?

For many, Friday is the gateway to freedom from pressures and stresses, from the accumulated difficulties and frustrations of the week that was. What a blessing is Friday: time to unwind, decompress, and recover.

For some, it is a time to catch your breath and calm down, time to regroup, to sort out any damage and refocus on blessings and positives that might have been lost in the scheduling. The opportunity to kick back and catch an evening with family and friends is special, an alternative to escape.

For others, the weekend offers escape. This seems to be the way for some, when pain is great. They do not feel like being with others and burdening them with their troubles. Who wants to hear? Who would understand?

Wine does not, as a rule, associate with aloneness, although some might be alone when they drink. Wine is for partnership: paired with food, shared with family, friends, and associates. Statistically, it is far from being the beverage of choice for someone wanting to be alone.

Wine is for toasting: expressing wishes for life, good health, friendship, and for so many facets of well-being and balance.

REFLECTION QUESTIONS FOR SIPPIN':

1. How do you re-energize, and at what points in the week?

2. How do you respond when you feel the inclination to escape?

3.

Sip 87: How Do Multi-Course Meals Enhance Courses of Life?

One of wine's contributions to enhancing a meal is the way different wines pair with different flavors, so a progression of wines can match each course served. Each course with its own wine provides a distinct taste treat, contributing to a whole feast.

Each participant comes to a meal such as this after a day sprinkled with activities, appointments, and tasks that often were experienced as disconnected fragments, lacking any unifying meaning—some important, some stressful.

How wonderful for mental, spiritual, and emotional well-being, to have time to kick back, relax, and muse about so many fragments—some significant, others not—as days fly by.

Pouring different wines, each enhancing a progression of courses, serves as a symbol to revisit the "courses" of your day and seek connecting threads that could transform today into a banquet. Here's to you and your day!

REFLECTION QUESTIONS FOR SIPPIN':

1. What lessons from one aspect of life could you apply in other areas?

2. How could you create more of a flow to your day and reduce fragmentation?

3. Just as different wines complement different foods, what different facets of your schedule could you restructure to allow for increased connectivity and less stress?

4.

Sip 88: How Does WineSpirit Connect With Larger Realities?

In worrisome times, WineSpirit offers more than escape from pressures and problems of everyday life. Yes, WineSpirit programs, or an evening of relaxed dining, will provide restful breaks. Yet, even more, a variety of interactive programs invites reflection on life's larger and deeper purposes.

In engaging questions of life meaning from varying perspectives, ranging from architecture to genetics, archeology to photography, history, poetry, romance, art, music, and health, the connection among them is a different understanding and expression of spirituality, encompassing all those areas, with the lead metaphor of wine and vineyards.

WineSpirit conversations accentuate *we*-ness: presenters and participants sharing nuggets of their life stories. When the late Jamie Davies commented in her WineSpirit video interview (part of the Spiritual Harvest Series) on the cooperative, community-like nature of wine growers, her son Bill added, "It is a community of giving."

Jamie and other elders and sages we have interviewed learned and taught appreciation for the land, reverence for the past, cherishing of relationships and growing new ones, and looking at life from new and different perspectives. Sharing life stories and journeys adds understanding to life purpose, in seeing how others live their values.

These kinds of exchanges add perspective on societal conditions, on where we are today as we look backward and forward. They are conducive to reflection on those causes we choose to address and support in contributing to a healthier world. We know we cannot enjoy quality of life when life itself is in danger.

Sitting still with a glass of wine, and sipping it slowly

provides a perfect setting for toasting in your heart for better times and a healthy world, restored; it is a pause that could energize and inspire a different attitude about the next day, and possibilities for contributing to a better and safer world.

REFLECTION QUESTIONS FOR SIPPIN':

1. How is quality of life affected for you when outside pressures mount?

2. What comes to mind of taking a break to relax and quietly reflect, changing your outlook and energy for the better?

3. Who do you like to be with in sorting through life values, and how often do you find time to do so?

4.

Sippin' Goes On...

WRITE YOUR OWN SIP

Now, it's your turn. We hope you are inspired to write a Sip of your own. And—if you are so inclined—we invite you to send it to our website at <u>execdir@winespirit.org</u>. With your permission, it may be published on the website or in the next edition of **Sippin' on Top of the World.**

Sip 89: TITLE: _____

Sippin' — YOUR WISDOM:

Sippin' — YOUR TOAST

<u>REFLECTION QUESTIONS FOR SIPPIN':</u>

1.

2.

3.

Sippin' on the Inside...

Sippin' the best of life—wine-based perspectives on life balance and well-being.

Sippin' on home to your spiritual and religious traditions and upbringing—seeing your sacred connections in new light.

Sippin' vintage bottles of life's significant moments, sharing unique stories and memorable times.

Sippin' words and images, engaging you in spirit, mind, and heart.

Different Sips for different folks, sharing Sippin' notes.

David White

About the Author

David White is co-founder and executive director of WineSpirit Institute for the Study of Wine and Spirituality. He is dedicated to bringing WineSpirit principles, connecting wine and spirituality with community building, into daily life. Toward that end, he has crafted some 150 of more than 170 Sips of WineSpirit — brief writings accentuating wine's contribution to vibrancy and meaning in everyday contexts, and the material upon which *Sippin' on Top of the World* is based.

In 1991 he left his position as rabbi of Congregation Kol Shofar in Marin County, California, to pursue an avenue to translate and apply principles for community building into secular settings. WineSpirit is one outcome of that search.

He also facilitates bi-weekly men's and women's groups exploring life balance in Napa, and serves as spiritual leader of Congregation B'nai Israel in Vallejo.

He was born and raised in San Francisco. He received a BA from the University of California, Berkeley, and was ordained as rabbi at the Jewish Theological Seminary of America with an MA in Theology in 1975. In 2002 he was awarded an honorary doctorate from the Jewish Theological Seminary of America.

Father of Joshua and Elana White, he has been married for 30 years to his best friend and life inspiration, Sharon L. Cohn.

Printed in the United States
146966LV00002B/1/P